PRAISE FC
DO YOUR BEST COACHING

"*Do Your Best Coaching* is a great, useful addition to the field of coaching for practitioners of all levels! Utilizing their own coaching experiences over many years, Hess and Daley offer coaches ways to bring heightened intentionality and presence to their work. New coaches will find practical approaches on how to cultivate successful coaching engagements, while experienced coaches will find practical tips and innovative ways to refresh their coaching approach."

—Pam McLean, PhD, MCC, Founder and Chief Knowledge Officer, Hudson Institute of Coaching

"A terrific guide for all coaches! Full of useful tips and practices that are brought to life with real coaching stories we can all relate to and learn from. Well-written and researched, *Do Your Best Coaching* will quickly become a critical resource for coaches new and seasoned!"

—Dr. Marshall Goldsmith, *Thinkers50* #1 Executive Coach and New York Times bestselling author of *Triggers, Mojo,* and *What Got You Here Won't Get You There*

"I love teaching coaching, but my students often have questions about how to manage the coaching relationships. I now have the answers! *Do Your Best Coaching* is a guide for coaches to manage everything from securing contracts to graciously ending relationships … and handling the sticky situations in-between. Full of examples, tools, checklists, and relatable stories, it is an essential resource you will continue to refer to throughout your years of coaching."

—Dr. Marcia Reynolds, MCC, Author of *Coach the Person, Not the Problem*

"In *Do Your Best Coaching*, Hess and Daley make an important contribution to the field of coaching. If you aspire to be a great coach, this book is a must-read. It provides a very thorough and practical guide to successfully navigating every aspect of a coaching engagement. Read it mindfully and take the opportunity to push pause while you reflect on how you are engaging your clients and how you can, with increased rigor, intentionality, and deep presence, add more value to your clients."

—Bob Anderson, Founder and Chief Knowledge Officer, The Leadership Circle, Co-Author *Mastering Leadership* and *Scaling Leadership*

"Authors Julie Hess and Laura Daley bring their presence and truth as they share their experiences, and distilled learnings, in service of offering an 'Intentional Engagement Framework' to support and inspire coaches, at any level, to bring deep value to their work. This is a book that is sturdy in its practicality while grand in its call for the devotion of service that our coaching clients hope and deserve to find."

—Dorothy E. Siminovitch, PhD, MCC, Author, Coach, Speaker, Director of Training for Gestalt Coaching Program-Istanbul/Toronto

"*Do Your Best Coaching* is essential for executive coaches. It offers a smart, thoughtful approach to managing engagements brought to life through stories, practices, and examples. It also captures the experience of internal leadership coaches and provides them with applicable insights and considerations that are often missing from coaching books."

—DeAnne Aussem, Managing Director, Well-being Leader and Founder of PwC's Leadership Coaching Center of Excellence

"Finally, not just a new coaching tool but the whole toolbox needed to build a great coaching engagement—*Do Your Best Coaching* is a powerful guide for coaches to create the conditions to draw out their clients' very best. With a framework and stories that are compelling and pragmatic, the authors have made a rich, robust contribution to our profession."

—David Peck, Partner and Americas Executive Coaching Practice Head, Heidrick & Struggles

"Do Your Best Coaching offers useful insight into coaching for coaches as well as anyone who works with coaches in a leadership development capacity. HR professionals will benefit from this insider's look at coaching engagements, learning what they can expect and how their organizations can best benefit from the coaches serving them."

—Brigitte D. Lippmann, HR Leader, Marriott International

"What a joy this book will bring to all coaches who continue to lean into personal and professional development. It is a treasure trove of ideas, experiences, lessons learned, and ideas for 'how' from two remarkable and distinguished coaches. The authors provide a road map rich with descriptive details of possible processes and approaches for the coaching engagement. The authors share the depth and breadth of what they have learned in a format that is readily accessible.

"It goes beyond any specific methodology or competencies and captures the practicalities and essence of coaching. It sets out possibilities, with comprehensive examples, for the coach to consider, reflect on, and adapt to their ways of being. There is a resonant balance between the relationships between the client and the coach, the relationships with the sponsor, and the coach's own preparation and reflections. It is an essential new resource."

—Dr. Kathryn M. Downing, D.Prof, PCC, JD, Executive Coach and Coaching Supervisor, Galileo Coaching

"*Do Your Best Coaching* is essential for new and experienced coaches working with organizational clients. The writing is clear, examples are abundant, and the authors offer a sound guide for ethical and professional coaching."

—Francine Campone, EdD, MCC, Accredited Coaching Supervisor,
Editor (Americas) International Coaching Psychology Review,
Past Director Evidence-Based Coaching Program Fielding University

"*Do Your Best Coaching* offers coaches an entire collection of best practices for successfully conducting a coaching engagement from start to finish. This easy-to-read and well-organized toolkit can be used by coaches to increase their conscious competence and set themselves and their clients up for success. Julie and Laura succinctly offer the wisdom too often learned after years of trial and error. I highly recommend this book as a resource for coaches who are beginning their practice or simply want a tune-up."

—Kathleen Stinnett, MCC and Certified Coaching Supervisor, Author of
The Extraordinary Coach: How the Best Leaders Help Others Grow

"You can learn core coaching skills in any number of good programs. But learning how to conduct a multi-month coaching engagement that helps a client achieve real change is another matter. Coaches typically gain insight and mastery into this over a period of years and have had few resources to guide them—until now. *Do Your Best Coaching* is a sensible, much-needed book that provides a framework and step-by-step suggestions for carrying out a successful executive coaching engagement.

"Ranging from aligning sponsors to managing your own emotions and behaviors in the process, Hess and Daley offer practical ways to shape coaching engagements effectively. I wish I'd had this book 15+ years ago—it would have prevented some scraped knees and face palms. I'm glad to have it as a resource now."

—Michael F. Melcher, Executive Coach, host of the Career Stewardship podcast, and author of *The Creative Lawyer: A Practical Guide to Authentic Satisfaction*

"In *Do Your Best Coaching*, Hess and Daley have captured both the architecture and the heart of a successful coaching engagement. The Intentional Engagement Framework integrates practical considerations for optimizing a coaching engagement from start to finish with the essential relational considerations that make all coaching effective and fulfilling. The tips, tools, and nuanced considerations provide a road map that can be adapted for coaching engagements in a variety of settings. Whether you are a new or experienced coach, this book will polish your practice and inspire you to be your best self and do your best coaching!"

—Debra Gerardi, RN, MPH, JD, PCC, Executive Coach and Hudson Institute of Coaching faculty

"*Do Your Best Coaching* is a gift to the field: practical, clear, with tools and models in the service of helping clients while providing the coach with a map from start to finish. That's no small order. The Intentional Engagement Framework provides the structure, and the discussion on presence wraps the ideas with the depth they deserve. Thank you, Julie and Laura, for putting this out to the world of coaching."

—John Schuster, Executive Coach, Founder Schuster-Kane Alliance, Author of *Answering Your Call* and *The Power of Your Past*

"A must-have for new coaches and a valuable tune-up for those of us who are more experienced. *Do Your Best Coaching* is filled with important, actionable content that coaches can apply immediately to their practices."

—Kathy G. Gallo, Executive Coach, Founder and CEO, Goodstone Group

"*Do Your Best Coaching* is not only a great resource for coaches, offering practical and thoughtful guidance, it's also an incredibly valuable read for HR and Talent professionals involved in coaching and developing executives and leaders. It provides a rare inside look into how coaches work, and sets the standards and frameworks for an organization's expectations of coaches partnering with them."

—Cara Bauer, PhD, Global Head of Human Resources at Kite, a Gilead Company

"Insightful and practical, *Do Your Best Coaching* is what the field of leadership coaching has needed for a long time! Julie and Laura bring to life the questions, challenges, and opportunities coaches face as they navigate their work in supporting their clients. Through their Intentional Engagement Framework, they invite coaches to become more aware of how they coach and bring their best coaching to fruition."

—Muriel Maignan Wilkins, Paravis Partners Co-Founder, Host of HBR Presents "Coaching Real Leaders" Podcast, and Author of *Own The Room: Discover Your Signature Voice to Master Your Leadership Presence*

"A great resource for both new and seasoned coaches, in this book Julie and Laura have brought to life the realities and subtleties of how to manage engagements that will enable your best coaching."

—Julie Starr, Coach, Speaker, Author of *The Coaching Manual, The Mentoring Manual* and *Brilliant Coaching*

"*Do Your Best Coaching* is going to change the lives of so many coaches by reducing the confusion and heartache that can occur while navigating the coaching process. It's an incredible resource and contribution to the coaching community."

—Amy Su, Executive Coach and Author, *The Leader You Want to Be*; Managing Partner and Co-Founder, Paravis Partners, Board Member

"This is the book I wish I had when I was starting out as a coach! It is easy to read, highly applicable, and relatable. New coaches will breathe a sigh of relief, and as an experienced coach, it inspired me to try some new approaches. Many of the coach training programs are phenomenal at teaching people how to coach, yet it seems few of them prepare their students for many of the other aspects that lead to a successful coaching business. This book closes those gaps. It addresses sticky situations that most of us didn't plan on having, yet face frequently. Even now as a seasoned coach, I have found this book to be so helpful, and I use it frequently as my 'I'm not sure what to do about this' guide."

—Lisa Kaplin, PsyD, PCC, Speaker, iPEC Coaching Lead Trainer

DO YOUR BEST
COACHING

Navigating A
Coaching Engagement
From Start To Finish

BY JULIE HESS & LAURA DALEY

www.doyourbestcoaching.com
hello@doyourbestcoaching.com

Printed and bound in the United States of America

Library of Congress Control Number: 2022903952

Publisher's Cataloging-in-Publication data

Names: Hess, Julie, author. | Daley, Laura, author.
Title: Do your best coaching : navigating a coaching engagement from start to finish / Julie Hess & Laura Daley.
Description: Includes bibliographical references and index. | Naples, FL: DYBC Press, LLC, 2022.
Identifiers: LCCN: 2022903952 | ISBN: 979-8-9857629-2-1 (hardcover) | 979-8-9857629-0-7 (paperback) | 979-8-9857629-1-4 (ebook)
Subjects: LCSH Counseling. | Personal coaching. | Personal coaching--Handbooks, manuals, etc. | Executive coaching. | Leadership--Study and teaching. | Performance--Psychological aspects. | BISAC SELF-HELP / General | PSYCHOLOGY / Education & Training | BUSINESS & ECONOMICS / Mentoring & Coaching
Classification: LCC BF637.P36 .H47 2022 | DDC 158/.3076--dc23

ISBN:
Hardback: 979-8-9857629-2-1
Paperback: 979-8-9857629-0-7
eBook: 979-8-9857629-1-4

DEDICATION

To our husbands, Dan and Alec, who gave us the space and grace to work together incessantly, and only occasionally (and with humor) referred to themselves as "book widowers." And to Laura's daughter, Maddie, whose determination inspires her mom, and who brightened our Sunday Zoom sessions with her flybys.

ACKNOWLEDGMENTS

So many people have asked us "what is it like to write a book with a co-author?" Our immediate response is that we could not imagine doing it any other way. However, we also share how grateful we are to be supported by an amazing community of family, friends, colleagues and professionals who have offered their wisdom and support every step of the way.

To our early readers: Amira Leifer, Amy Su, Anders Engen, Cara Bauer, Francine Campone, Jason Miller, Julie Starr, Kathryn Downing, Kathy Gallo, Kelly Grogan, Kelly Ross, Lisa Kaplin, Pamela McLean, Pat Henahan and Seth Levenson. Thank you for the time and care you invested and the valuable notes you provided to us. The book evolved tremendously with your insights and offerings.

To our colleagues who generously shared their insights, successes, sticky situations and learnings: Ann O'Connor, Blaine LeRoy, Bob Anderson, Brenda Routt, Carol Tisson, Cassi Christiansen, Claire Thomas, David Peck, Debbie Daniels, Janet Boguch, Jill Kidd, Joy Leach, Julia Holloway, Kathleen Stinnett, Leslie Goldenberg, Lisa Johnson, Liz Congdon, Melissa Hammer, Meredith Persily Lamel, Michael Hudson, Mike Engsberg, Molly Rabenold, Muriel Maignan Wilkins, Nancy Liffmann, Paula Fagundes-Ventura, Romi Boucher, Russ Hall, Ruth Williamson, Sandy Smith, Susan Geear, Tina Jackson, Trish Anastos, Tony Jenkins. You helped us bring this book alive.

To our amazing team: Bethany Kelly, Frank Steele, Stefan Merour, Whisper Roys, Catherine Knepper, Becky Robinson, Diane Hess, and Michael Hess. Thank you for your expertise, patience and commitment to excellence. We feel privileged to have worked with and learned from the best!

And finally, to our clients. It's an honor and privilege to do the deeply connected work of coaching with you, and to learn and grow alongside you. This book reflects our work together and would not have been possible without you.

We are blessed to be part of so many vibrant coaching communities. We have had so many formal and informal teachers throughout the years that we cannot possibly include everyone here. We are grateful for every interaction, discussion and connection, large and small. Thank you.

Julie and Laura

CONTENTS

START HERE

OUR STORY

We met in the spring of 2019 at the Hudson Institute of Coaching's annual conference in Santa Barbara, California. We were about to begin working together at a client organization, and the conference gave us the perfect opportunity to meet in person, as Julie lives in Chicago and Laura is based in Philadelphia. In that conversation we learned that prior to earning our coaching certifications we had parallel careers in management consulting, organizational development, and leadership development. Each of us had then built our own executive coaching practices, and over the past two decades we have had the privilege of coaching hundreds of executives.

Fast-forward to the summer of 2020. We were navigating the pandemic and had developed a regular practice of connecting by phone while walking. One afternoon, as often happened, the conversation turned to coaching, and specifically the topic of sticky situations we had faced earlier in our coaching careers. Every coach has experienced challenges that distract from the actual coaching or lead to disconnects, such as client sponsors assuming they will have access to client assessments, or engagements drifting because there wasn't a coaching plan in place.

Our discussion expanded to the processes, conversations and tools we now used to support healthy coaching engagements—things such as an intake process and kickoff meeting, clear communication and boundaries with sponsors, developing a vision and a coaching plan and a meaningful closing process.

That afternoon our shared experience coalesced into what would later become the Intentional Engagement Framework. We realized that when we approached an engagement intentionally from the start, and consistently integrated these elements across the arc of a coaching engagement, we created the container necessary to build a meaningful coaching relationship and do the deeply connected work we believe leads to great client outcomes. And, as a bonus, the risk of finding ourselves in a sticky situation was greatly reduced.

Almost simultaneously, we wished aloud that we'd had a practical guide outlining this approach when we were beginning our coaching practices. We laughed and said we could write that book now and title it *We Made Mistakes So You Don't Have To!*

Over the next month we kept returning to the topic of intentional engagements and started to explore the idea of writing the book we'd imagined. It would be the practical guide we wished we'd had when we were starting out.

The project took off quickly, with daily conversations revisiting past sticky situations and sharing how we approached our engagements. To supplement our own reflections, we surveyed and interviewed dozens of other coaches, from newly certified to deeply experienced, and built in their expertise and the stories they graciously offered from their own sticky situations. During those discussions we discovered that although we conceived this book for new coaches, experienced coaches were curious about the processes other coaches use and were delighted when they could find a new approach or tip to strengthen their own practice.

HOW TO GET THE MOST FROM THIS BOOK

This is not a book about how to coach, how to have a coaching conversation, or how to build a coaching practice. There are many great programs and books that cover those topics. Instead we follow the arc of a coaching engagement from start to finish, using the Intentional Engagement Framework to illustrate the tools and processes we use and why. We invite you to use this book as a practical resource that allows you to consider and integrate what's useful into your particular practice. This will differ by coach, based on your style and preferences, the work you do, and the clients you serve.

We conclude with two chapters that rest outside the coaching engagement: "Your Presence Is an Intervention: Coaching Presence" and "You Are Your Own Best Tool: Ongoing Development for Coaches." Both are intended to be resources to help you consider how to care for and develop your most important coaching tool—yourself.

To bring to life the issues coaches face, we have created a story that threads through the book, following a coach, Andie, as she navigates a coaching engagement from start to finish. We have also included vignettes throughout the book to illustrate sticky situations. Andie's story and the vignettes are pulled from our own experiences and from true stories our colleagues generously shared with us. They have been anonymized and at times presented as a composite of various coaches' experiences to maintain confidentiality.

We also include excerpts from coaching documents to illustrate how to apply the concepts in the framework. Over the years we have benefited from many coaches who have generously shared tools with us. And over the years we have adapted these and shared them with others, who have then surely evolved and passed them along.

Therefore, we want to acknowledge that the excerpts included in this book have their roots in a collective community of work, and for that we are grateful.

As we built the appendix of this book to include the sample tools, checklists, and other useful resources, we discovered the book was becoming longer than we had intended. Early readers encouraged us to "right-size" our use of samples and compile all of the structures, checklists, templates, and coaching exercises into an easy-to-access reference. Thus, *The Intentional Engagement Framework Workbook* was born, a practical companion to this book.

A final thought before you dive in. As we wrote *Do Your Best Coaching* and engaged in discussions with our colleagues, we noticed that we were paying more attention to, and sometimes tweaking, our own intentional engagement. And our coaching strengthened. It was a great silver lining as well as "proof of concept." So we encourage you to engage with other coaches on the topics here so that we all continue to share ideas, collaborate on creating new approaches, and raise our level of coaching.

WHY INTENTIONAL ENGAGEMENT MATTERS

Intentional Engagement is the act of mindfully and consistently attending to the processes and tools that support a healthy coaching engagement. As the framing of a building creates the space within a structure, intentional engagement creates the space for the coaching relationship and coaching conversations. And, like framing, it is not what you should see when you look at a coaching engagement. When done well, intentional engagement runs seamlessly in the background, creating the container for you to do your best coaching.

Below are the four phases of the Intentional Engagement Framework, their components, and the impact of doing them well.

THE INTENTIONAL ENGAGEMENT FRAMEWORK

PHASE I: CREATING THE CONTAINER

Defining ways of working with your client and the organization, including establishing boundaries and confidentiality, all of which is essential to developing the safe space and trust required in a healthy coaching relationship (De Hann et al. 2016).

PHASE II: ESTABLISHING THE THROUGH LINE

Clarifying where the client is today, what future success looks like personally and professionally, and the changes that will help them get from here to there. Establishing a through line ensures alignment on coaching objectives and creates the freedom to pivot to emerging issues when necessary, without losing focus.

PHASE III: MAKING PROGRESS

Coaching clients as they work to make the changes they aspire to, while checking for alignment with both the client and the sponsor throughout the process. Great coaching coupled with alignment touch points leads to clarity regarding success and client progress.

PHASE IV: ENDING WITH MEANING

Supporting the client and the organization to reflect on the work that has been done, identify and celebrate the client's progress, and plan for the future. A strong finish sets up the client and the organization for a smooth transition out of coaching and into continued growth.

A NOTE FOR INTERNAL COACHES

Many of our most trusted colleagues are internal coaches working within large organizations, and we have often discussed with them the advantages (e.g., stability and health insurance) and challenges (e.g., bureaucracy) of coaching internally vs. externally. So it was important to us to make this book useful to those who coach in the same organizations that employ them.

Over the past year we interviewed a dozen internal coaches and leaders of internal coach programs. Our goal was to understand meaningful differences between the work of internal and external coaches and if those differences would impact how internal coaches use the material in this book. Through our conversations, we learned that much of what we had written about intentional engagement is applicable, without further explanation. It was also clear that parts of the book could offer internal coaches additional considerations for the unique aspects of their work.

Internal coaches typically have a mixed coaching portfolio (e.g., executive, team, onboarding, etc.) and have significant discretion in how they approach their coaching engagements. While a few organizations prescribe certain process elements and tools, such as assessment type, use, and timing, most internal coaches are free to manage their coaching process and choose the tools to use. Some other advantages our internal coach colleagues enjoy include:

- Being a member of an established community of coach colleagues
- Access to valuable development opportunities funded by the organization and often provided by the leading experts in the field of study (e.g., master classes, group supervision)
- Spending time on client work without the distraction of business development and administrative work.

However, it will come as no surprise that internal coaches have to navigate the systems in which they coach with a different sensitivity than external coaches. One colleague shared, "As an internal coach you need to deliberately and rigorously create the systems and boundaries because they are not as defined as they are for external coaches." This sentiment was further validated by another internal coach who offered, "An effective internal coach is vigilant around boundaries and defending the safety of the coaching space." Other colleagues discussed the pressure internal coaches can feel to produce results quickly and how that can lead to inadvertently rushing the intake process and identification of coaching goals.

Internal coaches also discussed the value of developing a coaching culture in an organization. Establishing a coaching culture means there is a shared understanding of what coaching is, how it is used, and the conditions required for success. When this is in place, internal coaches report that it is easier to handle issues that arise.

Another important differentiation is in the type and duration of coaching engagements. Many internal engagements follow the process we illustrate, while others may be shorter and focus on specific issues, so internal coaches need to be able to flex their process and approach to meet the needs of a specific coaching engagement.

Below we share aspects of the coaching process our internal colleagues highlighted as more challenging or requiring additional sensitivity. With these, we offer the insights we gleaned from our internal coach colleagues and the parts of the book that provide helpful food for thought.

OPPORTUNITY	INSIGHTS FROM INTERNAL COACHES	WHERE TO EXPLORE
Managing confidentiality and boundaries	Internal coaches can face pressure to share client insights with sponsors or senior leaders, who have positional and political power, and who may not understand the importance of confidentiality and boundaries. Internal coaches are more likely to get caught out of context (e.g., stopped in a hallway) and asked to discuss a coaching engagement.	Chapters 1 & 2: How can you communicate the need for confidentiality and boundaries early in the process? How can you encourage sponsors to engage in three-way meetings to ensure coaching does not feel like a "black hole"? How can you prepare yourself to handle unplanned requests to discuss a coaching engagement?
Optimizing the intake process and creating the coach-client agreement	Intake is seen as a useful process but is used inconsistently. Internal coaches shared reasons spanning from familiarity with the organization or their client to feeling the need to "get right to it" and produce results quickly. This also impacts the coach-client agreement process, which can be "easy to breeze over in the haste to get started."	Chapter 2: Would an intake process enable you and your client to create a more robust foundation for coaching? How do you establish your coach-client relationship?

OPPORTUNITY	INSIGHTS FROM INTERNAL COACHES	WHERE TO EXPLORE
Taking time to explore vision and create a coaching plan	Internal coaches see the benefits of developing a vision but use the process inconsistently. Often coaching goals are identified and plans are created in the first or second meeting of an internal coaching engagement.	Chapter 4: How might slowing down the process create space to explore and generate insights? Would a vision exercise infuse aspirational energy into the coaching goals and plan?
Optimizing sponsor relationships and alignment	Sponsors may not understand their role in the coaching process and be more difficult to engage in the coaching process. Internal coaches cited reasons such as the perception that coaching is less of a priority when it is an internal transaction rather than a paid service, and company culture that does not hold sponsors accountable.	Chapters 4 & 7: How can you communicate the value and benefit of sponsor participation early in the process and gain agreement to participate in alignment and closing meetings?
Preparing for meetings	As employees, often with responsibilities beyond coaching, some internal coaches report challenges finding time to prepare and center for coaching sessions, as they do not have full control of their calendars.	Chapters 5 & 8: How can you manage your schedule to ensure you have time to pause and prepare prior to coaching sessions?
Closing the coaching engagement	Internal coaches find closing an engagement to be one of their greatest challenges. Some coaches cite the fluidity of internal engagements which may not have a clear, bounded time frame. Also, as there is no overt fee, clients have no motivation to let go of such a valuable resource.	Chapter 7: How can you communicate that closing the engagement and creating a sustainability plan is a part of a successful coaching engagement?

We thank our colleagues who shared their experiences so openly with us and hope that the themes and insights we share above further enhance this experience for our internal coach readers.

PHASE I
CREATING THE CONTAINER

CREATING THE CONTAINER

ESTABLISHING THE THROUGH LINE

MAKING PROGRESS

ENDING WITH MEANING

1

Securing &
Contracting

CHAPTER 1

PUTTING YOUR BEST FOOT FORWARD: SECURING A COACHING ENGAGEMENT

Andie Carlson was sitting at her desk gazing out the window at a gray March sky when an email with the subject line "Potential Coaching Engagement" flashed across her computer screen. It was from Melissa Hunter, VP of Talent Management for LMN International, a global manufacturing company. Andie had met with Melissa several months ago, but nothing had materialized. Now Andie felt a surge of excitement; it would be wonderful to get a toehold into a new corporation, plus she liked Melissa and what she had learned about the company. She quickly scheduled a Zoom meeting for the next day.

In the hour before the meeting, Andie reviewed her notes from their introductory meeting and revisited the company's website to learn more. Armed with information and insight, she took a few centering breaths and then opened her Zoom meeting room.

Fifteen minutes later, the meeting was over. It turned out Melissa was swamped and had another meeting to rush off to. In the brief time they connected, Andie learned about the potential client, Tom Revere, LMN's new VP of operations. Tom was viewed as a high-potential leader, but he was struggling with his new team. Andie didn't have as many details as she would have liked, but it seemed like a good fit, and she figured she would learn more as things progressed.

Later that day, Melissa sent a short email to Tom and Andie, suggesting they meet to talk about possibly working together. Andie was disappointed that Melissa hadn't provided any additional context. She knew that coaching at LMN was considered developmental rather than remedial, but she didn't know if Tom had received any feedback or reasons for engaging with a coach. All she knew was that she was one of three coaches he would be interviewing.

Well, no matter—she'd get all those details during her chemistry call with Tom. She enjoyed these initial calls with potential clients, and, by the end of the conversation they'd both come away with a sense of the work to be done, what it would be like to work together, and their fit as coach-client.

They met a week later via Zoom. Andie instantly liked Tom: He was smart, earnest, and funny, and after initial introductions he jumped right in. "I understand the company is investing in me with coaching," he said, "but I don't know anything beyond that. Can you tell me more about what I'm signing up for?"

"No problem, Tom," Andie replied. "It sounds like this will be your first experience working with a coach?"

"That's right," he said. "I've talked to other people's coaches when they were doing 360° interviews, but that's pretty much the extent of my knowledge."

"Then let's start by walking through a typical coaching engagement," she said.

Andie gave Tom a brief overview of the process, describing key steps and how they would work together. He asked a few clarifying questions and then they spent the rest of the meeting getting to know each other and discussing his development.

Tom was excited to be promoted but found himself in a difficult position. Not only had he never led a team of this size, but two of his new direct reports had been up for his position and resented being passed over. "I've tried everything, but I can't get them on board," he said with clear frustration. "I'm really worried Sydney is going to think she made a mistake in promoting me."

Recognizing the urgency of the situation, Andie asked Tom if he'd like to do some coaching right then on the issue of engaging his team. This was a technique she sometimes used in a chemistry call. Not only did it address an immediate need, it also gave the potential client an excellent preview of how coaching worked and what it would be like to work together. Tom readily agreed, and they spent the next 15 minutes focused on the situation.

It was all going well when Andie noted they were at the end of their meeting time. Tom thanked Andie and seemed genuinely pleased with the new ideas she'd offered, but he was late for another meeting and had to rush off. Andie felt great about their conversation, but uncomfortable with the meeting's abrupt ending. She wished she had managed the time better. That evening she sent a quick note of thanks to Tom, and then all there was to do was wait.

As the weeks went by with no word from Tom or Melissa, Andie started to worry that the chemistry call hadn't gone as well as she'd thought. She kept busy with other clients, but from time to time she felt a pang: In her haste to provide coaching on the spot, had she neglected some key element that would have sealed the deal? Had the rushed sign-off been detrimental?

Finally, a full six weeks later, Melissa called. "Congratulations, Andie!" she said. "Tom has selected you to be his coach. We're very excited to be working together!"

Andie was thrilled, but she kept her cool as they discussed next steps. Once again Melissa was in a rush, so she asked Andie to schedule an additional call with her to discuss formal contracting, and to follow up directly with Tom.

Energy soaring, Andie emailed Tom right away, sharing her excitement that they would be working together and offering windows to schedule their kickoff meeting. She then sent her availability to Melissa to schedule the contracting discussion, hoping she wouldn't need to chase her down.

Emails sent, she smiled, excited to have a new client. She set a firm intention to remember this experience. The long wait for Tom's decision had made her question her judgment. Remembering this experience would help keep things in perspective the next time a selection process seemed to drag on.

But now—full steam ahead! She couldn't wait to get started.

○ ○ ○

How you begin an engagement plays a significant role in its overall success. The first phase of the Intentional Engagement Framework, **Creating the Container**, focuses on the activities and discussions that enable you to ensure alignment on the coaching process and objectives, establish confidentiality and boundaries, and begin to establish a trusted relationship with your client.

Most coaching engagements begin with an initial inquiry, which often includes a request for a chemistry meeting designed to help both the client and the coach ensure that there is a good fit between them for the work to come. If the decision is made to move forward, a Coaching Statement of Work (SOW) must be developed and agreed upon.

How you handle the initial inquiry discussion and chemistry meeting is important, not just to secure the engagement but because these interactions set the tone for the engagement to follow. A clear SOW further establishes the structure and boundaries to support a healthy coaching engagement.

SECURING AND CONTRACTING A COACHING ENGAGEMENT: KEY ELEMENTS

* Initial inquiry discussion
* The chemistry meeting
* Coaching statement of work (SOW)

INITIAL INQUIRY DISCUSSION

The initial inquiry discussion can take place between the coach and the potential client, or between the coach and someone inquiring on behalf of the client (e.g., the client's hiring contact or engagement sponsor). Sometimes these roles are played by one person and in other cases by multiple people. Here is how we differentiate the roles and responsibilities:

Client. The person who is being coached.

Hiring Contact. An individual who makes the initial request for the coaching engagement and serves as a point of contact for administration, such as creating the SOW and invoicing.

This role can be filled by the client or the client's boss, but is often filled by someone in Human Resources or Learning & Development. In large organizations you may work with an individual hiring contact for many coaching engagements. If you are working with an individual directly, that person is also the hiring contact.

Engagement Sponsor. In corporate engagements, this is the individual who is championing and supporting the client through the engagement. This role is often played by the client's boss; however, certain aspects may be shared by an HR leader. Sponsors play an important role in a coaching engagement, as they provide organizational context and direction for coaching objectives as well as feedback and support during the coaching process (Pliopas 2021).

The initial inquiry discussion is your first opportunity to learn about the potential client and the organization. If the client reaches out to you directly, then the inquiry call may serve double duty as a chemistry call.

If the individual contacting you has experience with coaching, they may provide you with all the information you need to understand the potential engagement. However, if this information is not forthcoming, questions you might ask include:

WHEN TALKING TO THE POTENTIAL CLIENT	WHEN TALKING TO THE HIRING CONTACT OR SPONSOR
Tell me a little about yourself and what's motivating you to seek a coach right now. What might you want to work on with a coach?	Tell me a little about the potential client. What are the development objectives that have been identified and targeted for their coaching?
What feedback have you received from your boss or anyone else in the organization? How did you feel about the feedback?	Has the client received any feedback to date? If so, how did they respond to the feedback?
Have you received any development support from your company to date?	What type of development support, if any, has the client received to date?
What does your organization need from you in terms of business goals and performance in the next 6–12 months?	What does the organization need from this leader in terms of business goals and performance in the next 6–12 months?
Are you inquiring about coaching on your own initiative, or has it been suggested to you?	How has coaching been positioned with the potential client? How did they react?
What's your experience with, or perception of, coaching?	How does the organization feel about and use coaching (e.g., accelerating development of high performers or "fixing" underperformers)?
What role do you anticipate the organization playing in your coaching and what cultural norms do I need to be aware of to be as effective as possible?	What organizational norms do I need to be aware of so I can be as effective as possible?

If this is the first time you are working with an organization or an individual client, you'll want to share your coaching process and important aspects such as client confidentiality as early as possible. This proactive step is a great way to prevent future misunderstandings. For example, a hiring contact or engagement sponsor may not understand the importance of client confidentiality and assume that the coach will provide information on the client's progress or access to the client's assessment reports (Pliopas 2021).

During early discussions and while you are creating the SOW for the coaching engagement, you will have the opportunity to proactively share the need for confidentiality, while explaining that coaching will not be a "black hole" of secrecy. The process of clarifying and gaining alignment on the coaching relationship and confidentiality with all stakeholders* is essential to developing the trust a client and coach need to work effectively together (Alvey and Barclay 2007). Take this opportunity to discuss how you will keep the engagement sponsor involved in the process without violating client confidentiality.

*For our purposes, a stakeholder is a colleague invested in the leader's coaching.

Confidentiality Clarity

Jenny was contacted by the CHRO of a technology company to discuss a coaching engagement for a senior leader. During the initial inquiry call she discussed the engagement scope and process, but in retrospect, recalled that she did not specifically address the topic of confidentiality. "In hindsight I recognize the error," she said, "but I truly thought that this highly experienced CHRO understood that all coaching conversations are confidential. Also, my standard SOW includes very clear language around confidentiality." And yet, several months into the engagement she ran into the CHRO in the hall, who asked her specific questions about how the client was doing. "This was very uncomfortable because I was put in the position of either violating confidentiality or not meeting the CHRO's expectations," Jenny said. "I clarified what I could and could not share, but I know she was not satisfied, and that impacted our relationship. Now I'm better at setting rules up front. If I'm talking about a client with someone in the organization, the client is in the room. Or if the client chooses not to be there, they know when and where the discussion is happening, and we have discussed what I can share with the third party." This approach avoids misunderstandings and reinforces the trust in the coaching relationship.

Finally, this initial call is an important opportunity to establish your relationship with the hiring contact and engagement sponsor. Developing this relationship often enables senior-level access and support for the engagement as well as a conduit to insights on the organization, culture, and your client.

After you have concluded the initial inquiry discussion, follow up with a brief email that summarizes the discussion and next steps, and provide your bio. Your bio should include your contact information, experience, education, and certifications. Many coaches also include brief examples of recent coaching engagements.

THE CHEMISTRY MEETING

At the initiation of many coaching engagements, a potential client will speak with two to four coaches in order to experience a range of coaching styles and approaches. These 30-to-45-minute chemistry meetings are designed to help the client select the coach they believe they will work with best. This is essential, as the relationship between a coach and client is central to the success of the engagement (De Hann and Duckworth 2021).

Early in our careers, we often viewed these meetings as an opportunity to "win" a client—and if we were not selected, we viewed it as "losing." However, as we have gained experience, our perspective has evolved, which is why we have *not* called this chapter "*Winning* and Contracting a Coaching Engagement." We now approach chemistry meetings as an opportunity to meet someone new and enter into an open, curious discussion with them that encourages them to be their authentic selves. The reality is that not every client is a good fit for you, and likewise, you won't be a good fit for every client.

Chemistry conversations in which both parties show up as their authentic selves, and the potential client is given the chance to share their needs, give you an opportunity to determine if you'll work well together. Sometimes, there is a mismatch because the coaching need is not an area you focus on (e.g., career or wellness coaching), or perhaps you sense your coaching style won't be optimal for the client (e.g., they want more advising than coaching). Every now and again, you just won't "click," and that is reason enough to step aside, both for your sake and for the sake of the client. We've found that an open, encouraging approach in which we listen more than we speak is far more likely to secure clients who are a good fit than trying to "win" an engagement.

Once you have scheduled the chemistry meeting, take the time to research the company and the client. This can be as simple as a tour of the company's website and a review of the client's LinkedIn page. This background will help you identify things you may share in common, as well as questions you may use during your time together.

During chemistry meetings we try to give the potential client a sense of what it is like to work with us. We begin by asking what they'd like to get out of the conversation and then, based on their response, suggest a flow for our time together, such as: "Would it work for you if we spend some time getting to know each other, talk about what's bringing you to coaching, and then talk about the coaching process and how we might work together?"

Walking a client through your coaching process takes time but is essential to having a meaningful discussion about working together. If your chemistry meeting falls later in their selection process, they should already have a sense of the coaching process, so while you may offer some details about your approach, you can focus on getting to know the client. Finally, if you are the first coach they are meeting with and you've decided that you would like to work with the client, you might consider asking if you can connect again briefly before they've made their final decision, as they may have additional questions after speaking with other coaches.

In addition to process questions, be prepared to answer inquiries about your work, such as:

1. What's your coaching philosophy?
2. Have you worked with clients in my industry/function/situation before?
3. Can you give me examples of working with someone in my role?
4. Tell me about a coaching engagement that went well.
5. Tell me about a coaching engagement that didn't go well.
6. What makes for a successful coaching engagement?
7. How do you measure success?
8. How much of my time will coaching take?

A best practice for chemistry meetings is to offer coaching on a single issue for a brief time, as Andie did for Tom. This gives the client the opportunity to experience your coaching style and expertise. We approach this directly by asking, "Would it help to experience what coaching with me is like?" If they say yes, we ask them to share an issue that is on their mind and coach them for 10–15 minutes. We've noticed that when we use this approach, clients are more likely to select us, and we also have the opportunity to assess how it feels to work with the client.

Many coaches we know dislike selling, so closing a chemistry meeting may feel awkward. But, if you've approached this as a meeting where you are genuinely interested in getting to know the client, you will close it in the same way. Be yourself; if you enjoyed the conversation and think you would work well together, say that. You may also share that your priority is that they have the best coaching experience possible, so they should pick the right coach for them. Add that whatever their decision, you wish them well. We also let potential clients know we'd be happy to hear from them if they have additional questions during the selection process.

After the meeting, send a follow-up email to the client. Thank them for the opportunity to get to know them, reflect on some key moments from the meeting, and, if you feel you'd be a good fit, express again that you would enjoy working with them.

TOP TIP: On occasion you may be asked to coach a client without a chemistry call. While this can feel like a gift, you won't be able to check for fit or the client's desire for a coach. In these instances, we encourage the hiring contact or sponsor to introduce the potential client to other coaches, and we've gone so far as providing referrals. If they still proceed with you as the sole option, communicate your optimism that it will be a good fit, but that if it is not on either side, you will revisit the conversation. The exception to this is when there is someone who knows both parties well who is making the match.

The Gut Knows

Tony had been selected by an HR manager to coach Ron, an executive at a large life sciences company. While he was excited to have been chosen, Tony admitted to having some misgivings during the chemistry call. He remembered thinking, "Something's off here. Ron's answers are just a little too textbook." Even though his gut was telling him it was off, he decided to go forward, thinking that maybe Ron was just nervous, and that any issues would work themselves out as the engagement proceeded. Tony laughs ruefully when he reflects on that experience. "Nope! I should have listened to my gut. The coaching engagement was a nightmare. Ron was uncoachable, plain and simple. He was unable to listen to or act upon even limited feedback, and I struggled for most of the engagement until we decided to bring it to a close early."

At some point in your coaching career, you'll finish a chemistry call and sense a poor fit with the potential client. When this happens, share your reaction with the hiring contact and discuss the best way forward. Sometimes, that can mean waiting until the client decides, and letting the hiring contact manage the situation. Other times, you and the hiring manager may discuss under what circumstances you'd be willing to do the work, if selected. Another option is to explore who might be a better fit for the potential client, based on the chemistry conversation.

CREATING A STATEMENT OF WORK

Congratulations... you felt the client was a good fit, and they did too! Now it's time to formalize the scope and terms of the coaching engagement. The term contracting is used in multiple ways to describe both formal and informal agreements that occur throughout the course of a coaching engagement, so for clarity we will use the following terms:

Statement of Work. The formal, legal agreement a coach enters into with the client or the client's organization.

Coach-Client Agreement. An agreement between a coach and client that defines how they will work together, including expectations and roles and responsibilities. This may be oral or written and is not a legal contract. See Chapter 2.

Session Contracting. Discussions at the beginning or during a coaching session to ensure the coach and client are aligned on the objectives of their session. See Chapter 5.

A coaching SOW clearly documents the scope of work, articulating key elements of the engagement, including timing, cost, and confidentiality. The SOW serves to ensure alignment from the outset and provides support during the engagement if you find yourself in a situation where a client or sponsor is questioning any of these elements.

An SOW typically stipulates the following:
- Objectives for the coaching engagement
- Duration of the coaching engagement and number of meetings within this time frame. This may include a tune-up meeting two or three months after the conclusion of the engagement.
- An overview of your coaching process, including:

- How meetings will be conducted (e.g., in person, by phone, via videoconference, a hybrid)
- Which assessments, if any, will be used
- How you will keep the engagement sponsor informed and ensure organizational alignment (e.g., alignment meeting with sponsor and client)
- Confidentiality for all coaching sessions and assessment reports
- Cost of the engagement and expense policy
- Payment terms

Finalizing and signing the SOW can be a smooth, fast process or it can take an inordinately long time. If the process lags, communicate clearly that the coaching engagement cannot begin until the SOW is signed. It may be hard to postpone, as your client will be eager to get started, but if you begin without the signed SOW, it can be difficult to move the process along and you risk never getting the SOW signed.

TOP TIP: Use the SOW process to clarify who will be acting as the engagement sponsor, identify any other key stakeholders, and how you (and the organization) expect them to be engaged in the process. Clearly delineate sponsor alignment meetings in the SOW, including approximate timing, objectives, and desired outcomes. Also use this as an opportunity to stress the importance and expectation of coach-client confidentiality.

○ ○ ○

CHAPTER 1 TAKEAWAYS

Use the initial inquiry discussion intentionally to build relationships and to share your coaching process, highlighting important aspects such as confidentiality.

- ▶ Prepare for chemistry meetings so you are able to engage authentically and present your best self.
- ▶ Resist the desire to "win" clients via chemistry meetings. This approach may result in you acquiring clients that are a bad fit.
- ▶ Chemistry meetings are as much for you as they are for the client. Ask yourself if this is someone you want to work with and if this work will be interesting to you. Also ask yourself, "Do I have the right experience to coach this person?"
- ▶ Use the SOW process to establish clear expectations (e.g., engagement objectives, your coaching process, confidentiality) with the client and engagement sponsors.

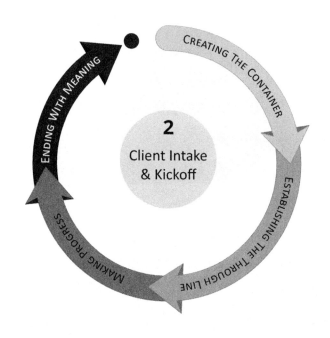

CREATING THE CONTAINER

ESTABLISHING THE THROUGH LINE

MAKING PROGRESS

ENDING WITH MEANING

2

Client Intake
& Kickoff

CHAPTER 2

STARTING STRONG:
CLIENT INTAKE AND KICKOFF

Andie sighed and closed her Zoom connection, ending her kickoff meeting with Tom. Their session had the same great connection as the chemistry call, but she couldn't help feeling some anxiety.

Andie had started with a clear kickoff agenda in mind, establishing how she and Tom would work together, going over the coaching process and discussing next steps to begin his 360° assessment. But instead Tom dove right into describing some of the issues he was navigating with his new team, and before she knew it, they were almost at the end of their time together. Andie rushed to fit in a quick conversation about working together and the assessment process, but she wasn't entirely sure Tom understood his next steps.

She was also regretting her decision to skip sending Tom her standard client intake form. Their initial call had been so rich that she felt she had a good understanding of him, but in retrospect she realized what she had missed. Sending the intake form signaled to her clients that they would begin the engagement by building their relationship and aligning on how they would work together. In its absence she found it harder to rein Tom in and set the foundation. Not to mention that she still needed that intake information, and now it felt too late to send the form.

And, she still hadn't been able to connect with her hiring contact Melissa, so she was working without a contract. Tom had been so eager to get started that Andie had not wanted to delay, but it was impossible to reach Melissa. She was trying to move the contracting process forward without annoying her and damaging their newly forming relationship, but now that Andie had started the engagement, she had no leverage. She knew they would get the contract done, but the loose end felt really uncomfortable. If this were one of her established client organizations she wouldn't be thrilled at the situation, but she wouldn't feel as anxious. In this case she did not have the comfort of knowing how this new organization operated, and she certainly didn't want to establish an expectation that she would work without a contract.

Andie stood up and stretched. She needed to take a walk and think about how to get this engagement straightened out before it was too late.

○ ○ ○

Throughout the kickoff and intake process, you continue **Creating the Container** for coaching, building a relationship with your new client, while establishing the structure and cadence for your work together. This is also the time to develop or deepen relationships and ensure that you and the engagement sponsor are in agreement about things such as the coaching process, and roles and responsibilities.

At times, this process can feel amorphous, as you may have started to develop these relationships and lay this foundation during the initial inquiry call. Often a chemistry call with a potential client can "click" and seem like the first coaching session. For clarity, we have chosen to define the start of the actual coaching process as after you have been selected as the coach. This serves as a healthy structure because many coaches, including us, have for one reason or another jumped from the chemistry meetings right into coaching and neglected to build a strong foundation.

However, even the most robust inquiry discussions or chemistry meetings do not take the place of a well-managed kickoff and intake process. Laying a strong foundation with clear processes, roles, and expectations can prevent unnecessary challenges and sticky situations later on.

BEGINNING A COACHING ENGAGEMENT: KEY ELEMENTS

- The kickoff meeting
- The client intake process

Note: While we make a clear distinction between the *kickoff meeting*, which is focused on how you will work together, and the *first coaching session/intake meeting*, which is when you will begin your work together, some coaches combine these meetings into a single session.

THE KICKOFF MEETING

Once you've been selected, start the kickoff process by sending an email to your client to let them know how pleased you are that you will be working together. Share that while you are finalizing the contract, you would like to schedule your kickoff meeting. This ensures that you will be ready to kick off as soon as the contracting process is complete.

The kickoff meeting is a 30-to-45-minute conversation designed to set you and your new client up for success by discussing how you will work together. Co-creating a shared model for working together by taking this time to align on key roles and expectations leads to significantly better client outcomes (DeChurch and Mesmer-Magnus 2010).

We often begin this meeting by sharing our end-to-end coaching process, particularly if we did not discuss it in our chemistry meeting, so the client knows what to expect. Often we use an illustration that begins with the kickoff meeting and includes key milestones such as the assessment process, organization alignment meetings with the engagement sponsor, and the closing process. To see a copy of the coaching process illustration we use with our clients go to www.doyourbestcoaching.com.

In addition to reviewing the coaching process and answering any questions, we introduce the coach-client agreement. As discussed in Chapter 1, many SOWs are between a coach and an organization on behalf of the client. With the SOW in place, it can be easy to assume you have covered your bases. However, because a coach has relationships with both the organization and the client, it is equally important to create an agreement between the coach and client (Hannafey and Vitulano 2013).

The coach-client agreement articulates how you will work together. It can be either written or oral and typically covers roles and responsibilities of the coach and client, logistics such as scheduling, and confidentiality. If you have created a statement of work directly with your client, you have probably already addressed this.

SAMPLE EXCERPT FROM A COACH-CLIENT AGREEMENT

Coaching is designed to create new awareness and understanding for the Client and help them focus on untapped abilities, insights, and energy to build new skills, and enhance professional development and personal growth. To achieve these objectives:

Coach's Role and Responsibilities
- The Coach will work together with the Client to schedule coaching sessions and to develop a coaching plan that addresses the goals identified and agreed upon.
- The Coach will involve the sponsors in the course of the engagement to collect feedback, and, in partnership with the Client, to align goals and share progress.
- Prior to using an assessment, the Coach will recommend tools in accordance with the organization's plans, preferences, and approach to assessments.
- The Coach will …

Client's Role and Responsibilities
- The Client is responsible for good-faith participation in coaching sessions, including identifying skills, behaviors, and goals for improvement; assisting with the design of assignments and practices as they apply to the coaching goals; practicing new behaviors or approaches; participating in exercises and simulations associated with implementation of the coaching plan; and observing progress throughout the coaching process.
- The Client will be responsible for …

Coaching Logistics
- Coaching sessions will be scheduled at times mutually agreed on by the Client and the Coach.
- Frequency of coaching sessions will be determined by mutual agreement of the Client and the Coach.
- All coaching sessions …

Confidentiality
Without revealing information shared in confidence, the Coach will encourage and support open dialogue and sharing between the Client and the sponsors, including …

Signatures

_____   _____

Client's Name   Date

_____   _____

Coach's Name   Date

NOTE: This sample agreement has evolved over time and was shaped by the examples coaches and organizations generously shared over the years.

We wrap up the kickoff meeting by ensuring we've covered the nuts and bolts of starting the engagement:

- Agreeing on the meeting cadence and timing
- Identifying important upcoming events that may affect coaching (e.g., board meetings, vacations, team off-sites)
- Scheduling your first coaching session, the intake meeting, and sharing that you will be sending some work for them to complete beforehand
- And, if you are beginning an assessment process, discussing the "next steps" to initiate it (see Chapter 3)

Every client is different, so be mindful of the balance between defining the process and expectations and establishing a connection and a relationship. For example, some engagements begin with a pressing need that must be addressed quickly (e.g., an emergent, challenging situation). You can be creative and flexible in how you meet the client's needs while also building a strong engagement foundation. If you omit this, you will probably find yourself circling back over the course of the engagement.

> **TOP TIP:** If you've not yet spoken with your client's manager, you'll want to set up a time to talk with them about the context for coaching. This is also an opportunity to share your coaching process and discuss the important role they play.

THE CLIENT INTAKE PROCESS

A client intake form is a document you send to your client in advance of your intake meeting to gather foundational information. When we interviewed coaches for this book, we were surprised to learn that there are as many intake processes and forms as there are coaches. Some coaches focus primarily on gathering basic data (e.g., contact information, professional history), while others use the intake to have clients begin to reflect deeply on their personal and professional life to date, using exercises such as a lifeline, a self-assessment, and reflective questions.

We include both categories of information in our intake form: basic data and self-reflection. It is a repository for the client's fundamentals, such as demographic information, contact information, including Executive Assistant (EA) information (if applicable), organization information including their role and function, an org chart if available, important meetings, deadlines, or scheduled trips, and so on.

But it's also a vehicle to gather valuable insights that help us begin to understand more about the client. Probing, self-reflective questions guide the client in reflecting on their career and life experience, all the way up to what brings them to coaching. These kinds of questions provide important insight into the client's world and their desired outcomes. It also provides a useful opening in early sessions to learn more about who they are, what has worked or not worked for them in the past, and how they would like to be supported and challenged.

The depth and length of your intake form should match your coaching style and the types of clients you serve. For example, certain clients may not have the time or patience for an extended intake form or may view it as too programmatic, while others would greatly value the experience. Create an intake form and process that best serves you and your clients. For example, for our most senior clients we often ask their EA to complete the demographic information and ask the client to simply reflect upon the questions prior to our session.

We each have a master intake form that we tailor to clients as needed. In addition to demographic information, questions to consider for your intake form include:

1. Why are you seeking coaching and why now?
2. What would be successful outcomes of our coaching engagement?
3. Have you experienced coaching in the past? How was it helpful?
4. What you need to know about the client to provide the best coaching, including their strengths, issues they encounter repeatedly, learning style, and how they like to be supported or challenged.

Sending an intake form to your client signals that you are thoughtful, planful, and invested in their development. In addition, the act of completing the intake form requires the client to pause and think about why they are engaging a coach and what success will look like. This shifts the client from a "waiting to begin" mindset to an "in process" mindset. Our experience is that clients who complete a robust intake form arrive at the first session with greater focus and intentionality.

We ask clients to send us their completed form prior to our first coaching session so that we have time to review it. However, we do not postpone this meeting if we haven't received the form. Instead, we consider it an opportunity to learn more about the client and what got in the way (e.g., workload, family issues, difficulty pausing to do the reflection).

There have been times when both of us have skipped or truncated the intake process, often because the chemistry meeting was so good we already felt a strong connection to the client. We have always regretted it.

Slow Down to Speed Up

Perveen and Anna had been a great fit from the first minutes of their chemistry call and spent much of the call discussing Anna's goals for coaching and how overwhelmed she felt given her workload and family responsibilities. She admitted she wasn't sure how she'd be able to make time for coaching and asked Perveen not to assign homework outside of the coaching conversations. Empathizing with her client, Perveen agreed, and proceeded without doing her usual intake process, substituting a quick chat to collect basic demographics. By the third conversation, it was clear that Perveen had done her client a disservice by skipping the self-reflection typically included in intake; she lacked important context and insight about Anna, and Anna resisted providing it during their calls, preferring to be action-oriented rather than "navel-gazing." They missed seeing a couple of patterns and mindsets that undermined Anna's intentions to change, so Anna made slower progress than she wanted.

Perveen took this lesson to heart and set an intention to explain to each new client the importance of the intake for setting the proper foundation for coaching work. The information it provides, and especially the self-reflection it engenders, helps clients achieve their goals more quickly and completely.

TOP TIP: There are many aspects to a successful client kickoff. Ensuring you have a reliable, repeatable process and tools in place will position you for success, particularly when you have more than one new client kicking off in the same time period.

CHAPTER 2 TAKEAWAYS

▶ Balance the process aspects of a kickoff with relationship-building so that you ensure you are meeting the client's needs and establishing a strong foundation for the engagement. You can be creative and flexible in how you accomplish this.

▶ Share your coaching approach highlighting key process steps, establish expectations of confidentiality, and clarify roles and responsibilities with your client. This early alignment reduces the risk of confusion or erroneous assumptions later on.

▶ A client intake process ensures that you have the information you need to successfully launch and manage a coaching engagement while shifting the client from a "waiting to begin" mindset to an "in process" mindset.

▶ It can be tempting to skip some of these steps based on a strong chemistry meeting, but don't. No amount of connection can take the place of your investment in creating the coaching container.

STARTING STRONG

PHASE II
ESTABLISHING THE THROUGH LINE

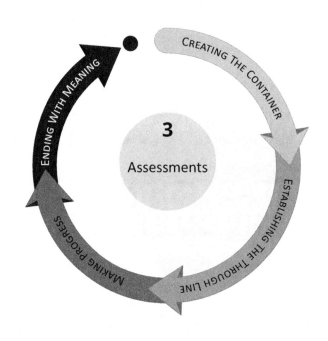

CREATING THE CONTAINER

ESTABLISHING THE THROUGH LINE

MAKING PROGRESS

ENDING WITH MEANING

3

Assessments

CHAPTER 3

BUILDING AWARENESS: ASSESSMENTS

A ndie had some backtracking to do with Tom during their next meeting to clarify how they would work together, agree on expectations, and discuss the steps to initiate the assessment process. It had turned out okay—they had covered all the necessary information during their allotted time—but the whole thing felt clunky to Andie.

After what she thought of as "Kickoff 2.0," Tom put together a participant list for his 360° assessment process and sent it over. When scoping the engagement with Melissa, they had decided to start with an interview-based 360° assessment. Andie felt comfortable with the timing, as she and Tom had built a connection quickly, he was eager for feedback, and he had not expressed anything other than the normal apprehension that comes with a 360°.

Later that day Andie did a cursory review of Tom's list and realized he had not asked his manager, Sydney, to weigh in. It made her wonder if this was an oversight or if it indicated something about his relationship with Sydney. She made a mental note to check on this during their next session.

Andie loved conducting 360° interviews in a new organization. In addition to listening for Tom's strengths and development areas, it was always interesting to learn about how an organization functioned and to understand its culture. The interviews went well, with clear themes emerging. Honestly, the worst part was just scheduling everybody. Sometimes her calendar felt like a game of Tetris.

Then came the hardest part, writing the darn thing. Over the years Andie had refined her assessment process. She knew if she left all of the analysis to the end, she would feel overwhelmed, so she processed notes periodically instead of waiting until all the interviews were complete to identify emerging themes and areas she might want to explore in her remaining interviews. She had also created a standard report framework with introductory language and a structure focused on top strengths and opportunities for growth. But no matter what she did to refine her process, it was always a challenge to wrestle so much data into an impactful and meaningful narrative. She usually went through a one-pound bag of M&Ms while she got the thing down on paper!

It was hard to predict how clients would react to 360° feedback, so Andie knew that it was best to arrive at the debrief ready for any-thing. She had carved out time to get grounded and to think about how she wanted to be present and hold space for Tom. She had also prepared Tom for the debrief in their prior session, engaging him in a discussion about how he best received feedback and what he might be anxious about.

Thankfully, Tom's debrief went pretty well. He was affected by the constructive feedback, but still able to hear it and ask some great clar-ifying questions. At the end of the session, they agreed that he would reflect on the assessment report and think about the development opportunities he wanted to focus on during their engagement.

○ ○ ○

Simply put, clients engage in coaching to make change happen. Some want to accelerate their development as leaders, others to support moving into a new role successfully, and others to address a challenge that has been holding them back. Still other clients may wish to focus on changing specific behaviors or patterns in their lives that influence their happiness and success.

The second phase of the Intentional Engagement Framework is **Establishing the Through Line,** and the first component of this phase is Assessments. Assessments offer clients the opportunity to build self-awareness, increasing their understanding of who they are and how they are perceived by others. They can vary widely (we'll look at specific types below), but in general, they're any process or tool that identifies and describes a person's strengths, characteristics, opportunities for growth, or other unique aspects. By more clearly understanding their current state, clients are better able to envision what it will take to successfully make the changes they desire. The insights that assessments generate are important inputs into a client's coaching plan, which we discuss in Chapter 4.

ASSESSMENTS: KEY ELEMENTS

- Selecting assessments
- Timing of assessments
- Confidentiality
- Preparing to debrief assessment results

SELECTING ASSESSMENTS

As you develop the scope of your engagement with your client, you will probably discuss the important role assessments play in coaching and the different types of assessments available. You will help determine what assessments to use and when, based on the client's particular situation and the organizational context. Be aware that occasionally an organization will have a standard assessment approach for coaching engagements that you will be asked to follow.

Common categories of assessments include:
- 360° assessments (e.g., 1:1 interview-based, online survey such as The Leadership Circle Profile, or a hybrid of the two)
- Preferences & Styles (e.g., MBTI or DiSC)
- Motivations & Derailers (e.g., Integrative Enneagram-iEQ9, RHETI or Hogan)
- Strengths/Values (e.g., VIA or Strengthsfinder)
- Specialist (e.g., EQ in Action, Be Well Lead Well Pulse)

When we asked colleagues which assessments they use, the most common response was "It depends on what the client needs." However, as these discussions continued, coaches often revealed that, like us, they use a foundational approach and customize the approach based on what will serve the client best.

The most common assessment executive coaches use is a 360° assessment (360°), which gathers confidential feedback from a client's boss, peers, direct reports, and other stakeholders, and organizes the feedback by theme. This is probably due to the impact this type of assessment has on coaching outcomes. Research shows that integrating a 360° into a coaching engagement can increase leadership effectiveness by up to 60 percent (McCarthy 1999). A 360° enables a client to build self-awareness by understanding how their organization perceives their impact, strengths, and opportunities for improvement. It clarifies the work they can do to be even more effective and to understand what "great" looks like. This increased awareness illuminates potential blind spots and provides guidance on the path forward. We explore the 360° further in Chapter 3[+].

Some coaches choose to marry a 360° with other assessments that provide insight into a client's preferences, personality, or motivations such as the MBTI, Hogan, or iEQ9. These insights help a client look inward, understand more about who they are, and how they can use that knowledge to support the change they want to make.

We are certified in one or more assessments from each of these categories, and enjoy the learning created by using them in our work. We do not use a standard battery of assessments in a single coaching engagement. Here are some of the factors we consider as we craft an assessment strategy for a client:

1. What are the objectives for the coaching engagement and which assessment(s) will best support the client in achieving these objectives?
2. What are the client's change intentions and their degree of awareness?
3. Where are we in the coaching process?
4. Is the client nervous or resistant to a 360°?
5. What data already exists? What assessments have already been done?
6. What expectations exist around coaching engagements at the organization? Do all coaching engagements include a 360°, and if so, is there a prescribed approach?
7. Does the organization have a preferred assessment tool that must be used? Are there any assessments that are prohibited?
8. What is the budget for assessment?
9. What is the organization's performance review cycle and how might that affect timing for an assessment?
10. Is the organization in the midst of an activity (e.g., annual planning or budgeting process) that is consuming the time and attention of the participants you need to interview?

An additional factor to consider is your access to and experience with various assessments. Some assessments are complex and require both training and practice to master. We each have a few assessments that are our "go-tos." We rely on them not only because they lead to significant client awareness and meaningful coaching conversations, but also because we have gained experience with them and understand their respective nuances, and thus can help the client harvest the full value from the assessment.

Once you have considered the factors above, you are ready to create the optimal assessment strategy for your client.

TOP TIP: When considering which assessments you want to invest in learning, look to both your coaching community and to your client organizations. Most coaching colleagues will freely share the tools they use and why, as well as those they were certified in but rarely use. In addition, many client organizations invest significant time in researching tools and assessments, and you can benefit from their vetting process.

If you are asked to or wish to use an assessment you're not certified in or not well versed in, engage someone who is highly skilled in the tool to administer it and conduct the debrief with you and the client. Then you can bring the insights into the coaching work.

TIMING OF ASSESSMENTS

Assessments are used at different stages of the coaching process for different purposes. Early in the process they serve to build self-awareness and insights that can shape the coaching objectives.

During the process they can provide additional insight or a new lens to look through. And as you conclude, they can provide data on both the coaching process and the client's progress (Smewing and McDowall 2010).

GETTING READY

Before or during the kickoff meeting you may learn that feedback is already available in the form of performance reviews or past assessments. If so, ask your client to send you copies to review as these are a rich source of data and a great, early opportunity to understand more about your client.

Occasionally a client believes they have all the data they need to jump to creating a coaching plan. But before moving ahead, it is worth exploring this with the client to ensure you have the right information and insights. For example, is the available information current? Is it relevant to the client's role today? Does it capture a well-rounded view of the client or a narrow slice?

Without the right assessment data, you and the client risk:
- Setting off in the wrong direction: The client works on what they want to work on and makes progress, but it's not what the organization needs from them.
- Setting off not knowing the destination: The client doesn't have a clear idea of what the finish line looks like and is frustrated when their idea of success is different from the organization's.
- Setting off believing the coach is an omniscient guide: The client relies on the coach having the answers to what they should work on, what success looks like, and how to make the organization happy with the outcomes of coaching.

Generic Labels vs. Actionable Feedback

Thomas had been told in a recent performance review that he needed to have more gravitas in order to be considered for a promotion. In exploring this with his manager, he heard things like "increase executive presence" and "be more assertive with peers." His manager offered an example or two, such as the SLT meeting in which Thomas didn't speak up. In fact, he had spoken up twice in that meeting, but his manager didn't remember it that way. Thomas took up the offer to work with an executive coach, and as they talked about his goals, he had a difficult time articulating the concrete changes he wanted to make. He and his coach realized they didn't have enough data about the skills and behaviors the organization wanted to see from Thomas and decided that a 360° would be valuable in providing clear feedback that they could use to shape his goals and coaching plan.

EARLY IN THE ENGAGEMENT

Conducting assessments early in an engagement increases a client's self-awareness and helps the client develop a robust coaching plan that leverages their strengths, addresses their development opportunities, and factors in how they are most likely to approach change. However, we also weigh this benefit with the level of trust and comfort we have established with our client. This is particularly true for a 360°. Some clients may be anxious about the prospect of gathering 360° feedback, and we discuss that anxiety with them as we talk through the process. In certain instances, a client's anxiety may be overwhelming, and it makes sense to pause and do some coaching around this until you have developed the level of trust and understanding needed to move forward with the assessments.

MID-ENGAGEMENT

Another approach is to use additional assessments later in an engagement to create new insights or generate further momentum for the change the client wants to create. That said, not all clients will benefit from this; some are better left continuing as they are. Here are some situations we've come across that are ripe for using an assessment mid-engagement:

CLIENT SITUATION	POTENTIAL TYPE OF ASSESSMENT
A client's need surfaces during coaching, and assessment would aid further exploration. For example: A client realizes they have difficulty working with specific peers who communicate and work differently from them.	Preferences & Styles (e.g., MBTI, Social Styles)
You and the client (and perhaps the sponsor) agree that an additional assessment could be useful, given information that emerged from the 360° or initial goal setting.	Specialist (e.g., EQ in Action, Be Well Lead Well Pulse)
Coaching momentum or progress seems to have slowed. Introducing another lens through which to look at things can add variety, awareness, new ideas, and questions.	Motivations (e.g., iEQ9, RHETI) Strengths/Values (e.g., VIA, StrengthsFinder) Specialist (e.g., EQ in Action, Be Well Lead Well Pulse)
Having worked together for a few months, you have a hunch a client would benefit from working more deeply, becoming more aware of their values, triggers, tendencies, and motivations.	Motivations (e.g., iEQ9, RHETI) Strengths/Values (e.g., VIA, StrengthsFinder)

NEARING THE END

We conclude many of our engagements with a progress assessment which gathers information from the client's colleagues to illustrate where they have made progress during the engagement and where there are ongoing opportunities. It also serves to remind key stakeholders what the client is working on, enabling them to better notice change and provide ongoing support.

A progress assessment can be interview- or survey-based. We keep it tightly aligned to the client's goals and involve the client in deciding who to include in the assessment.

If you choose to conduct a progress assessment, begin three or four weeks before the end of the engagement, as clients appreciate debriefing the progress assessment well ahead of their final coaching conversation. This ensures they have support to make sense of the results and incorporate it into their Ongoing Development Plan. We offer further guidance in Chapter 7.

Assessments Across an Engagement

Roberto started coaching a high-performing VP, Camila, who was having a hard time connecting with and understanding the impact of her words and actions on her team, who were unmotivated and stressed out. She also didn't know what she should work on in coaching to address the issue. Roberto and Camila agreed that doing an interview-based 360° up front would help shed light on her struggles and inform the coaching. As they built trust and Camila made progress over a few months, Roberto raised the idea of diving into this further by doing an EQ assessment, which Camila agreed to so she could learn more about herself. Finally, as they neared the end of the engagement, Camila was eager for Roberto

---

to conduct a progress assessment so she could understand how her team now experienced her. She was curious—had her hard work paid off? The progress assessment answered those questions (yes!) and provided Camila with a great foundation for her Ongoing Development Plan to help her focus on sustaining her progress and continuing her development.

CONFIDENTIALITY

Regardless of the assessments you use, you'll want to proactively create safety for your client and those contributing to the assessments by clearly addressing confidentiality. It's important to agree on who will have access to the assessment results (in the near term and over time) and on expectations about sharing the results once they are delivered to the client.

We prefer that all assessment results belong to and are managed by the client. This ensures that the client has agency to share results in the way that best supports their development efforts.

For 360°s there are some additional considerations:
- Will participants' names be listed in the results?
- Will participants have anonymity? (For example, will comments be attributed? Will comments be edited to protect anonymity?)
- If using a quantitative tool, are there enough participants in any rater category that the results don't highlight any single person's input, apart from the manager's?

Our strong position is that the content of any 360° be non-attributed, providing anonymity for the participants. The only exception is that in some cases, we ask the client's manager if an aspect of their feedback may be attributed to provide appropriate context and weight. This enables a coach to gather the most candid feedback, both positive and constructive. It also minimizes the risk that a relationship might be damaged if a client is surprised by feedback that is attributed to a colleague.

Some organizations believe that the HR leader or sponsor should have access to the assessment results, because HR is responsible for the organization's coaching investment (Pliopas 2021). If that is the case, it is critical that there is full transparency with the client. They must know before starting the process that others will have access to the results. Failure to be clear with everyone involved (client, client's sponsor, and anyone else involved in the engagement contracting) can lead to uncomfortable situations and erode trust (Alvey and Barclay 2007).

— DEBRIEFING ASSESSMENT RESULTS —

WHEN TO SHARE THE ASSESSMENT RESULTS/REPORT

Coaches usually have discretion in deciding if they want to introduce the assessment results to the clients ahead of a coaching conversation or as part of a coaching conversation. We start by thinking about what's in the best interests of the client based on:

Client preferences. Some clients prefer to read and reflect on the results before engaging with you as the coach. If your client is introverted, they may benefit from being able to read and privately process the results before meeting. Meanwhile, clients who are more extroverted, with a preference for thinking aloud, may get more value talking through the results with you first, then reflecting on them.

The content of the results. Do the assessment results provide a consistent narrative or a more varied/complex narrative that may be easier discussed? Do the results align with previous conversations about the client's interest in coaching or are they quite different?

Environmental context. Are you able to sit down in person with the client to review the results together, or will you be relying on a video conference or phone conversation? How would being able to see or hear your client's initial response to the results serve the coach-client relationship?

PREPARING YOURSELF FOR THE DEBRIEF

Despite the hundreds of assessments we've delivered, we can still feel nervous going into a debrief. If you're using assessment results early in the engagement to create awareness and shape goals, then this is one of the first and most important interactions with your client. It can accelerate the trust and rapport between coach and client, or it can derail it. Preparation for both you and your client will contribute to a successful conversation.

Several days ahead of the debrief, we review the results, make notes for ourselves, and think about how to frame the results in a way the client can absorb them.

It's important to have a clear point of view on the key themes of the assessment and their impact. Offering a laundry list of feedback doesn't accelerate a client's awareness or the goal-setting process. We encourage you to have a perspective on the highest-priority, highest-leverage insights to accelerate the client's development. At the same time, keep in mind that an assessment is just data, and that data will never fully define your client. It is helpful to check in with yourself on this and, if you notice that you are starting to view your client and the coaching solely through the lens of the assessment, ask yourself how you can broaden that lens.

As you ready yourself to share the results, consider what in the assessment resonates with you and where you might get triggered to overempathize or rescue a client in distress, or conversely, to pull away. Most coaches we know have practices for centering and managing themselves so they can be fully present with the client as they process the feedback:

- Joe notes the emotions that surface when he rereads the final version of the assessment report; this helps him process and release them ahead of the debrief.
- Clara uses a breathing practice before and during the debrief to stay centered and present to her client's experience.
- Nguyen has a mantra that she taps into when she feels herself wanting to rescue the client from their discomfort, especially if tears show up.

Finally, consider what you know about the client and their relationship to feedback: Do they regularly give and receive feedback? Are they aware of what they want to work on in coaching? Have you been told by others that they can be defensive?

PREPARING YOUR CLIENT FOR THE DEBRIEF

We help our clients get ready for an assessment debrief by asking them the following questions ahead of the meeting:
- What do they want to learn from the assessment?
- What do they expect to hear?
- How are they feeling about the assessment debrief?

This insight helps us better prepare to deliver the results effectively.

We also invite them to collaborate with us on where/how to have the conversation: in person or virtually? If in person, choose a different location than the office, or at the very least, not in a glass-walled conference room. We want to co-create the conditions that will make it as comfortable and productive a conversation as possible.

SUPPORTING THE CLIENT'S EXPLORATION AND INTEGRATION OF ASSESSMENT RESULTS

You'll rely on your coaching skills to support the debrief conversation, as well as your knowledge and experience with the tool itself.

Here are some consistent practices that we use in debriefs:
- Recall the intention behind doing the assessment and what the client can gain from it.
- Be prepared to define jargon/terms in the assessment that might not be clear to the client.
- Support the client in their own interpretation of the results— how do they make meaning from them?
- Realize that some clients may not grasp all the assessment points immediately. It can take additional reflection time, or it may not happen at all.
- Ask questions to help your client notice and process their reactions.
- Anticipate and manage your own reaction if the client becomes emotionally triggered by the assessment results.
- When the client is ready, ask them to articulate their insights from the assessment and how it informs the work they're doing in coaching.

Assessments, when skillfully and empathetically deployed, can offer the client a greater understanding of themselves and how others experience them. This helps them envision the shifts and changes they want to make in coaching and how best to achieve them.

CHAPTER 3 TAKEAWAYS

▶ When done well, assessments create greater self-awareness and insights for your client, and offer them a broader organizational perspective.

▶ There are countless choices regarding assessments in a coaching situation, such as what to use, when to do it, and who to include. Be thoughtful and take care early in the coaching process to optimize the assessment strategy for the client and the organization.

▶ Timing is critical. Using assessments before trust is established can derail a coaching relationship.

▶ Assessment results can provide an overwhelming amount of data if not presented well. Take time to carefully identify themes and high-priority insights.

▶ Deliver the results and insights in a way the client can hear and integrate them.

▶ Support, but do not rescue the client through what can be difficult awareness building.

▶ Continue to reflect on the possible use of assessments throughout the coaching engagement to increase coaching impact.

▶ Your client is more than the assessments you've completed; if you notice that you are starting to view your client only through the assessment results, consider how you can step back and take a broader perspective.

CHAPTER 3+

360° ASSESSMENTS: A DEEPER DIVE

W e spent countless hours discussing, writing, and rewriting the chapter about assessments. We felt that the topic of 360° assessments deserved additional attention but we were stymied on how to provide rich, actionable information without re-creating work that has been done beautifully by others or moving into how-to-coach territory. In this "+" chapter, we cover process elements that we have not seen addressed elsewhere, directing you to other great resources for certain aspects. And admittedly, this may be the one place in this book where we drift into "how-to-coach" territory.

360° ASSESSMENTS — A DEEPER DIVE: KEY ELEMENTS

- Determining the approach
- Implementing the approach
- Debriefing the 360° results

DETERMINING THE 360° ASSESSMENT APPROACH

As we discussed in Chapter 3, time, cost, and organizational context are important factors not only for selecting assessments but also in determining your approach. Once you have explored these factors, you will be ready to select a 360° approach.

There are three main approaches to gathering and reporting 360° feedback:
- An interview-based 360°
- A survey-based online 360° (online 360°)
- A hybrid approach augmenting an online 360° with an abridged interview-based 360°.

The following table highlights key considerations for each approach:

PROS/CONS OF 360° ASSESSMENT TYPES AND APPROACHES

	INTERVIEW-BASED	SURVEY-BASED ONLINE 360°	HYBRID (Online survey and 4–5 interviews)
UPSIDE	Offers in-depth insight, as the coach can elicit nuance, substance, and examples. Creates a dialogue with participants that the coach and client may leverage in coaching. Ensures actionable feedback. Creates greater stakeholder investment in the success of the client.	Provides quantitative data that some leaders trust more than qualitative data. More participants can be included without increased cost. If proprietary, may be aligned with their organization's leadership competencies or other frameworks. Lower investment	Some benefit from both approaches: ability to involve more participants cost-effectively, and being able to dive deeply with a handful of participants to tease out nuance and action-oriented input. Moderate investment

	INTERVIEW-BASED	SURVEY-BASED ONLINE 360°	HYBRID (Online survey and 4–5 interviews)
DOWN-SIDE	Takes more time for the coach. A greater investment of time and thought for stakeholders. Limits on total number of participants for reasons above. Higher investment.	May not offer important nuances to help client understand fully.	Abridged interview-based approach means a small risk of missing an important interview or insights.
WHAT IT LOOKS LIKE	8–10 interviews are enough to provide a full picture for the coach; you may choose to exceed this number if excluding someone will affect the process or the client.	Online 360's that require participants to respond to a set of questions typically take 15–20 minutes to complete. Examples are: • The Leadership Circle Profile • The Leadership Effectiveness Analysis • CCL's Benchmarks	4–5 interviews Online 360° Consider the order of assessments: interviews after online survey provide an opportunity to explore key themes for additional nuance and actionability.

In most of our engagements, we use an interview-based 360° with eight to ten participants, or a hybrid approach integrating four or five participant interviews with an online 360°. A standalone online 360° can provide rich information, but we miss the extra depth provided by even a handful of supporting interviews. In very specific circumstances, a minimum viable approach includes two or three interviews to inform our work and guide the creation of the coaching plan, typically when a client was very recently assessed or the coaching is part of a cohort development program.

IMPLEMENTING THE 360°
ASSESSMENT PROCESS

Once you have determined your approach, both you and your client have roles in starting the process. We use a 360° process overview document to help our clients understand the steps, including logistics, timing, and their role. Many clients are anxious about asking for and receiving colleague feedback. Talking through the process provides you with another opportunity to work through any concerns and answer open questions.

INITIATING A 360° ASSESSMENT

Regardless of your approach, you will begin by having the client select participants and request their participation.

Selecting participants is a collaborative process. Clients will benefit both from your guidance about who to select as contributors and their manager's input to the list. We typically provide the client with our recommendation on the number and type of participants, then discuss the importance of having a diverse slate of participants and being strategic about who's included. For example, if a client:

- Has four direct reports but only asks you to interview three, ask why and explore the message they may be inadvertently sending by excluding one individual.
- Includes only peers and senior managers despite managing a team of eight, discuss the impact of missing out entirely on upward feedback, or essentially doing only a 270° assessment.
- Lacks diversity (e.g., excluding a gender, a race, a level in organization or a function) on the list, raise the observation and talk about what implicit bias that may bring to the assessment results.

- Regularly works across functions and hasn't added key peers across the organization to the list, get curious with the client about why and what impact it would have on the assessment if the coach proceeds with the list as is.

Once the participants have been identified, the client will invite them to participate. When the client does the inviting, they create connection and agency, and increase participation. We provide the client with draft language they can tailor for an email (or speaking points) to simplify this process for them.

Sample Draft Email

As part of my professional development, I'm working with an executive coach, Jose Guillen. To help me make the most of the coaching experience, Jose (cc) is conducting confidential 360° interviews with a number of colleagues.

Given our work together, it's important to me to include your perspective in this process. I hope you'll be willing to schedule a 30-minute conversation with Jose. He'll want to hear your thoughts on and get examples of:

- My contributions
- My strengths
- My opportunities to be even more effective
- Specific suggestions for leveraging strengths or being even more effective

Your honesty and candor are very much appreciated. The information you share with Jose will be held in confidence.

Jose is cc'd on this email and will be following up with each of you via email to schedule individual interviews.

CONDUCTING A QUALITATIVE 360°
ASSESSMENT: INTERVIEWS, DATA ANALYSIS,
AND WRITING THE ASSESSMENT REPORT

There are great resources available that walk coaches through the process of conducting a qualitative coaching 360°. Our favorite is *Fearless Feedback*, authored by a team of coaches: Rebecca Glenn, Penny Handscomb, Amy Kosterlitz, Kathleen Marron, Kelly Ross, Lori Siegworth, and Timothy Signorelli.

- For guidance on conducting 360° interviews, we recommend Chapter 5: Structure and Conduct Interviews.
- For guidance on analyzing the data and writing the feedback report, we recommend Chapter 6: Create Stakeholder Feedback Report.
- For guidance on debriefing the feedback report, we recommend Chapter 7: Conduct Leader Debrief.

Following are tried-and-true practices we've incorporated into our 360° process over the years:

CONDUCTING INTERVIEWS

The first few minutes of an interview. The individuals being interviewed might feel curious or anxious about why they've been included and how their comments will be used. We start each conversation by offering context for the interview and how the output will be used. We outline confidentiality and invite any questions about the process. In starting with these things, we establish rapport and trust and are able to address any concerns. It may seem like it takes too much time out of the interview, but when we have skipped this step, participants sometimes offer less direct and specific feedback.

Use a structured interview guide. Ask more or less the same questions of all interviewees and collect interview notes in an equally structured way. This allows for easier processing on the back end.

The last minutes. We ask two questions before we thank them: (1) Is there anything we have not covered that they think is important to know so we can best support the client's development? and (2) May we follow up should we have any questions as we begin writing the report?

PROCESSING INTERVIEW NOTES AND DATA ANALYSIS

Process as you go. Waiting means we may not notice until it's too late that we haven't collected enough on strengths, or we may not have specific examples to bring a particular opportunity to life. These days, we schedule time to process a few interviews at a time. However, as you process early interviews, be careful not to get attached to your early insights as this can create an unconscious bias that can influence how you question and listen in remaining interviews.

Circle back. If there is feedback that's highly conflicting or requires additional context, we reconnect and test hypotheses with the client's manager.

There are as many ways to process interview notes as there are coaches. Over the years, we've tried different approaches and are constantly evolving our approach to tracking themes and coding notes. Following are several approaches shared by colleagues:

- Luke captures all of his interview notes in a single document, organized by participant. Once finished with interviews, he reads the notes, then puts them aside and outlines Strengths and Opportunities, and any frameworks he might want to use. Then he codes his notes accordingly and enters them into the report. He organizes themes based on how often they came up in the interviews, with special weighting sometimes given to a manager's feedback, or by referencing the organization's leadership competency model.

- Jennifer types her notes directly into an Excel spreadsheet, using a different worksheet for each question. She then categorizes the statements (e.g., strategic, delegation, communication) and creates a pivot table that lets her view the comments within the different categories as well as the density of statements.

- Carol types her interview notes, using the same questions for each. When she completes the interviews, she collates all of the responses for each question, then color codes them by theme (e.g., yellow for communication, etc.) to get a visual sense of the weighting of the various themes. She either shuffles the order of comments for each question to remove any participant pattern or she organizes them by themes if themes are really clear across the feedback.

WRITING THE FEEDBACK REPORT

Prioritize themes and offer a clear point of view. 360° results can be overwhelming if they're not prioritized and well supported. We analyze our data to look for themes that are mentioned most frequently or are most critical to the leader's success. Offering more than three or four strengths and three or four opportunities risks diluting focus on what is most important.

Data is critical. Be cautious about including an opportunity that's not well supported by multiple contributors or examples.

Coach's voice vs. organization's voice. Our client organizations hire us because we've worked with hundreds of leaders over the years and can support the organization in clearly articulating its collective perspective on the client. This means we use our judgment in how we organize the data, the themes that are most important to include, and the most salient and instructive examples and advice to support those themes. When a doubt arises in us around "Is this too much of my perspective?" we remove whatever triggered that doubt from the written report. We may return to it during the debrief.

SUPPORTING THE CLIENT TO PROCESS AND INTEGRATE THE 360° RESULTS

Your approach here depends on whether you've shared the results ahead of the debrief. In either case, you'll want the debrief to encourage reflection and emerging awareness, through your skillful coaching. We start the conversation by explaining our role: what we are here to do and how we can support them in receiving and making sense of the assessment results. Depending on our sense of the client, we might also normalize the experience of receiving feedback by sharing some typical scenarios:

- This may be a lot of feedback all at once for a client and it may take multiple reads or conversations to work through it.
- The client may find themselves agreeing with some feedback and disagreeing with others, and that's natural.
- There may be feedback that isn't clear or is contradictory.

With most clients, we talk them through a high-level summary, and then review each strength and opportunity in more detail, guiding the conversation with questions that elicit their reactions, questions, and potential actions.

While no two debriefs are alike, here are some common scenarios we've experienced in our practices, and thoughts on how to approach them:

A lot to process. If the client doesn't regularly get feedback (and sometimes, even if they do), it can feel like a lot of information to process. In this case, you might suggest they take some time to review the written document, encourage them to note questions or reactions, and reconnect with you after a day or two.

Needing clarity. Clients may be puzzled by themes or specific examples and struggle to interpret them. You can add context if you can maintain confidentiality, and you can also suggest that the client explore this further with their manager.

Interpreting conflicting data. Conflicting data happens, and exploring it together is helpful. Be curious about the data and determine if there is a useful hypothesis to consider.

When deep emotions arise. Clients may experience distress with the 360° results. From a structure and tools perspective, ensure you've centered yourself ahead of the conversation and know your own tendencies in the face of strong emotions.

Organizational view differs from client's view. This can be a challenging experience for the client, especially if the organizational view is less positive than their own. We begin by helping them understand the distinction between their intentions and others' perceptions. This enables them to consider how to shift their behavior, so their intention is clear to others. Other ways forward include giving them time to process the emotions that come up, and when the time is right, reminding them of the support they have from the organization, their manager, and you to shift things.

Off and running. Clients may eagerly receive the feedback and already be moving to action. Great! In this case, we're ready to share a set of questions to help them fully reflect and talk about next steps in the process of goal setting and action planning.

The Problem with Assumptions

Ken's client, Karim, had come to his senior executive role at a FinTech company from consulting. Ken assumed that Karim, like many consultants he had worked with in the past, would be comfortable receiving feedback and processing it quickly. What Ken hadn't understood was that in the four years Karim had been at his current company, he'd received almost no feedback apart from progress on his business goals. During the debrief, Karim started to shut down; it quickly became clear that he was receiving more developmental feedback in this conversation than he'd received in his entire time at the company. It was also clear that he was uncomfortable showing any emotion, and Ken sensed it might be because they were seated in a large, glass-walled boardroom. Ken paused their conversation to share his observations. Together, they agreed it was important to take more time for this conversation and to change venues. Karim quickly found a private conference room and rescheduled his next meeting so he and Ken could continue more comfortably exploring and processing the feedback and his reactions to it. After the session concluded, Ken noted what he learned from the experience so that he could change how he prepared for future 360° debriefs.

WRAPPING UP THE DEBRIEF SESSION

Some clients process their 360° quickly and are ready to move to the next step; others require more time or clarity. Regardless of how you work with your client to wrap up the 360° debrief conversations and move them toward goal setting, it's important to cover the following ahead of creating the coaching plan:

- Support the client to continue reflecting on the feedback. We do this in different ways based on the client's style and preference. We may share a list of questions and ask them to reflect and respond in writing; other clients may prefer to leave us a voicemail with their top takeaways. Still others may just appreciate the request to come to our next meeting prepared to share their insights.

- Ensure the client has understood the feedback and that any outstanding questions are captured for further exploration.

- Reconfirm the agreement about what's happening with the 360° (who sees it or doesn't see it based on what was agreed up front with the client and organization).

- Suggest the client send notes of thanks to people who participated in the 360°.

- Agree to a quick call or email to touch base in the week following the debrief to see how the information is landing and what next steps the client is ready to take.

POST-DEBRIEF SUPPORT

We support the client in considering what they will share from the 360° results, how and with whom. This varies based on the organizational expectations, the client's situation, and level of comfort:

- Ned wasn't comfortable sharing the full 360° results; instead he wrote up a summary of the results and what he learned from them and shared that with his manager in the alignment meeting.

- Ines was working on demonstrating appreciation and being more collaborative; she shared several of her insights from the 360° in her thank-you notes to participants and encouraged them to offer her informal feedback in these areas over the next several months.

- Jacob shared his full 360° results with his manager because he was curious about some areas and wanted to explore them further with her. He also shared a summary of the findings with his three direct reports because he was relying on their regular informal feedback as he worked on his goals.

- Johanna, a high potential known for skillfully engaging others in her development, shared the full results with her manager and her HR business partner as part of the alignment meeting; she also shared her most important insights and her coaching goals with her team in their next meeting and asked for their support.

A 360° can be enlightening and meaningful for the client when thoughtfully selected and well-debriefed. As described in *Fearless Feedback*:

> "The fundamental lesson regarding stakeholder feedback debriefs is to make sure you as coach treat this as a coaching session, and not as a delivery of the results from an assessment tool. Feedback is personal. It needs a personal, empathetic touch in order for the message to be received and accepted."

This is an excellent reminder for debriefing a 360°, or any assessment that you've carefully selected and incorporated into your work with a client.

RESOURCE

- Fearless *Feedback: A Guide for Coaching Leaders to See Themselves More Clearly and Galvanize Growth,* Glenn, Handscomb, Kosterlitz, Marron, Ross, Siegworth, & Signorelli

CHAPTER 3+ TAKEAWAYS

▶ When done well, 360°s offer crucial organizational perspective on how the client is seen and how the client can strengthen their leadership and have a greater impact on their organization.

▶ There's no one-size-fits-all approach to 360°s, so take the time to consider the organizational and client-specific context to develop your approach with each client.

▶ Create time to thoughtfully prepare ahead of the debrief and take steps to prepare your client as well.

▶ Support your client to think through how they wish to communicate with the individuals that contributed to their assessment. This is an opportunity to strengthen relationships and influence how they are perceived as a leader.

CREATING THE CONTAINER

ESTABLISHING THE THROUGH LINE

MAKING PROGRESS

ENDING WITH MEANING

4

Vision, Goals, & Plan

CHAPTER 4

CHARTING THE COURSE:
COACHING PLANS—VISION AND GOAL SETTING

A ndie was caught off guard when Tom arrived at their session apologizing for not making progress on his draft coaching plan. With other clients, this wouldn't surprise her, but Tom had done such a great job of creating his leadership vision, and then considering his assessment results through that lens, that she assumed he would have no problem drafting his coaching plan.

Now they were in the middle of the session working to flesh out the plan, and Tom was struggling to articulate his goals. She could feel an urge to get directive and move the process forward and winced involuntarily, recognizing a familiar pattern.

She hated to admit it, but her early approach to goal setting and coaching plans had been driven by her own need to add value and "fix" her clients. She would zero right in on addressing the presenting coaching need and the key development opportunities that emerged in the assessment. She got impatient with her clients as they crafted their coaching plans and would step in and write them herself because she believed she was better able to frame the issues.

That had been a tough time in her practice. Everything had felt hard, and for good reason; her approach meant her primary focus was on fixing problems, which felt heavy. And she felt that heaviness intensely because she was more focused on her clients' goals than her clients were and ended up working harder than they did. As Andie gained experience, she realized that this was not how she wanted to work. It wasn't good for her or her clients.

So she was happy that she noticed this urge now because she could actually do something about it. She did not want to drive this process; Tom needed to own it. She leaned back in her chair and took a deep breath, intentionally changing her energy.

It was time to bring him back to his leadership vision—"I will become a leader who articulates a compelling vision and strategy for my function and engages and develops my team so we can achieve it together"—which sat at the top of the empty coaching plan. "Tom," she said, "let's pause and reset. Think about your leadership vision. What are the two or three things you must do to become that future leader?"

It took a while, but by the end of the meeting Tom had drafted three goals that were clearly linked to his vision. Now he felt energized and ready to build a plan to achieve these goals.

○ ○ ○

Early in coaching engagements, we ask clients to complete a vision exercise, creating a picture of the leader they aspire to be. Their leadership vision becomes the compelling destination for the work we are doing and imbues the development opportunities that surfaced in their assessment process with greater meaning. We also know that clients who engage in future-focused conversations like this are more committed to the goals they set and have a stronger relationship with their coach (Passarelli 2015). Finally, this aspirational approach ensures that the coaching, even when initiated by a developmental need, is energizing and compelling to your client.

The insights generated through the assessment process plus the client's leadership vision guide the development of the client's goals and coaching plan, which are the final components of **Establishing the Through Line**. This through line supports the coaching by ensuring that sessions focus on what is most important, instead of what is top of mind, and that sessions don't meander without getting deep traction in any area of development. It may feel counterintuitive, but a through line creates alignment and clarity that actually provides you and your client with the freedom to address emerging issues without losing sight of the overall coaching objectives.

In some instances you may find that a client or sponsor is so focused on getting to work that they want to skip or rush through creating the vision and the coaching plan. If this happens, share the business case for this work: the strongest coaching plans are rooted in a clear and compelling vision, and the process of developing the plan ensures the client owns the plan and understands how its elements will lead to achieving their vision. A coaching plan is also useful to achieve organizational alignment with the engagement sponsor. The client's draft coaching plan is the foundation of the sponsor alignment meeting, which is designed to ensure that you, your client, and their sponsor are aligned on the focus of the coaching.

Finally, a coaching plan helps you and your client see where progress is being made and where you may be getting stuck. This perspective enables you to celebrate and sustain progress, while pivoting where necessary. It also provides the structure to seek feedback during the engagement and when you complete a progress assessment at the end.

VISION AND GOAL SETTING: KEY ELEMENTS

- Creating a leadership vision
- Integrating the leadership vision with assessment data and themes
- Setting goals
- Creating the coaching plan
- Sponsor alignment on the coaching goals and plan
- Setting up informal alignment through stakeholder* feedback

*For our purposes, a stakeholder is a colleague invested in the leader's coaching.

CREATING A LEADERSHIP VISION

We often discuss the concept of creating a leadership vision in our chemistry meetings as it is core to how we coach. This also influences our questions in early sessions as we are getting to know our client more deeply. These early discussions begin the process for our client, putting them into an aspirational mindset. We build upon this mindset by asking our client to complete a leadership vision exercise. This is frequently done by the client in parallel while we conduct their assessment process. The timing is intentional; we do not want our client's vision to be influenced by external feedback that they hear during the assessment debrief. The leadership vision should begin with the client and be built from their self-knowledge, interests, and desires, not by the leader others want them to be.

The vision exercise we offer our clients guides them through a series of questions designed to elicit their values, interests, and aspirations as a leader. It then shifts, placing the client into that vision by asking questions about what it is like to be that future leader. For example:

- What are the key values that define your leadership?
- What are your signature strengths as a leader?
- Why do others want to be led by you?
- Why do your counterparts want to collaborate/partner with you?

The exercise then shifts to the conditions necessary to achieve this:
- What do you need from the organization in order to be successful?
- What do you need to ensure you are not only leading for the best of the organization but for yourself as well (e.g., balance, boundaries, principles…)?
- As you honestly consider the leader you are today and the environment in which you live and work, what obstacles or gaps would prevent you from realizing the future vision you've described?

Ultimately, the client is asked to write a leadership vision statement that describes the leader they wish to become and why.

As with all exercises, you will tailor the experience to your client. While the preceding questions are a good sample set, we often adjust the exercise, adding or removing questions based on who the client is and the work they are doing.

If the client comes to the session prepared to talk about their vision, we help to explore and refine it. If the client resists putting pen to paper, this is a good entryway to understand what is deterring them from looking to the future. There may be important history getting in the way, or they may struggle to do this work on their own and need some help. When this happens, we walk the client through the exercise, asking the questions and engaging in discussion to help them develop their vision. The only aspect of this process that is non-negotiable is that you *cannot* do it for the client. This vision exercise *must* be client-driven; it must originate and develop from their heart.

Clients often work on this exercise in phases before it is complete, and they may return to it in the middle or at the conclusion of the engagement to update it based on what they've learned. As with most coaching exercises, the completed document is useful, but the process of completing the document is where the true value resides. This exercise often surfaces new awareness of strengths as well as challenges. It also fuels development as the client can more clearly see what they need to do to make their vision a reality.

SAMPLE LEADERSHIP VISIONS

- **Mai.** I will be a leader who effectively navigates a matrix organization by skillfully listening and adapting my communication style as needed to influence its direction and outcomes.
- **Jon.** I will become a more visionary and innovative leader who engages others in the vision, using change management skills to rally the organization around it.
- **Anika.** I will lead my team to become the best version of ourselves by actively living our core values, striving for excellence, and delivering results that matter.
- **Claude.** I will become a leader who thinks, works, and communicates more strategically, increasing the value I deliver to the organization, and preparing myself for broader leadership roles.

INTEGRATING THE LEADERSHIP VISION WITH ASSESSMENT DATA AND THEMES

As your client is creating their leadership vision, you are completing their assessments. As discussed in Chapter 3, you will share the assessment data and themes in a debrief session, and it will probably take time for your client to consider and integrate what they have learned. When your client has fully processed what they've learned from the assessment, it's a great time to ask them to think about the feedback relative to their leadership vision. What are the shifts they believe will enable them to become that future leader? These shifts form the basis of the client's development goals. At the conclusion of this discussion, the client typically has identified a few potential goals for coaching.

Future-Proofing the Vision

Colleen was coaching Ian, an IT leader in the transportation industry. Ian was trusted in the organization for his deep knowledge of how the organization worked as well as his ability to execute under pressure. If he were in charge, everyone knew it would get done on time and on budget. Ian's leader, the CIO, had placed him into his succession plan and had provided feedback on areas to expand his leadership capabilities so he could meet the needs of the role. While Colleen was conducting 360° interviews, she asked Ian to create a leadership vision describing how he would bring his unique strengths to the future CIO role. Later, when Colleen and Ian reviewed the 360° results, they noticed a consistent theme. The Executive Leadership Team talked about how IT needed to be different in the coming years to ensure the company remained competitive. Ian had touched on this in his vision, but the added assessment data caused him to spend time considering how the rapidly changing industry would change the role of a CIO and how he would need to lead. Ian's vision, combined with his assessment data, added a new dimension to the process he had not foreseen. Colleen supported him in translating this into a robust coaching plan with compelling development goals that aligned to the future needs of the organization.

SETTING GOALS AND CREATING A COACHING PLAN

Once we have explored the intersection of the assessment data and the client's leadership vision, it is time to create the coaching plan. As we reflected on our work with clients, we recognized a few basic principles:

- The plan is anchored by the client's leadership vision, and each goal in the plan is in service of achieving this vision. This adds meaning to the goals and minimizes the risk of them becoming tactical, untethered "to-dos." For example, a leader may have a coaching goal focused on *increasing delegation*. In the absence of a vision, this goal could feel uninspiring. However, it becomes compelling when it is part of a coaching plan to help a leader achieve a vision of shifting from an execution-oriented leader to a strategic leader.

- Work with two or three goals maximum—any more and you risk diluting focus and not gaining traction.

- Goals focused on *starting or becoming* are more effective than goals focused on *stopping or stifling* a behavior (Payne 2007).

- Support the client to use their growing self-awareness to create experiments that leverage their strengths and how they are wired.

- As the coaching continues, new insights will emerge. Expect the plan to evolve in support of the client's expanding awareness (Kauffman and Coutu 2009).

- The client owns the coaching plan; the coaching plan does not own the client. In other words, the coaching plan illustrates the client's aspirations and the changes they believe will help them get from "here to there," but it is not a document to be slavishly adhered to in coaching sessions.

In most cases, we share the coaching plan template with the client at the end of the vision-assessment integration discussion and ask them to draft something before our next session. This builds on the momentum of the session and the high-level goals that emerged. We stress that this is a draft and they shouldn't get too bogged down in getting it "right."

We have seen many coaching plan templates over the years and have found that the most effective format contains the following:

- The client's leadership vision statement. An overarching statement that captures the key elements of who the client aspires to be as a leader. It might take the form of a declaration or a from-to statement.
- Two to three specific, prioritized development goals. However, if a client has created more than three goals, do not discard the goals with a lower priority. Often a client will make such progress on an early goal that you can then add another to the plan.
- For each goal include the following:
  - Potential experiments or actions the client can take to support the change.
  - How making the change will benefit the client, the people who work for him or her, and the organization.
  - Who/what can support the client during the process (e.g., check in with them and give them feedback on the spot)?
  - What's going to be hard about this—what challenges can the client see already?
  - How progress will be measured. In other words, how will we know if the change is happening?

Before we meet with the client to review the draft plan, we review their assessments and vision as well as notes from recent sessions. This enables us to notice if something important that was referenced in conversations or that surfaced in the assessments is missing so we can ask curious questions.

At this point it is important to remember that this is a *flexible process*, so work with the client wherever they are. Some will come to the next session with a robust draft; others will arrive and sheepishly share that they didn't get to it. Coach them wherever they are in the process. If they have made significant progress, talk through the goals, behaviors, and metrics, expanding upon the plan while surfacing important insights into what is most meaningful to your client, as well as any fears or concerns. If they have not made progress on the plan, walk the client through the coaching plan, asking them questions and engaging in discussion to help them develop it.

Analogous to the vision exercise, if a client comes to this session with empty hands, it may be tempting to step in and complete the template for them, particularly if the engagement sponsor is expecting to see a completed plan quickly. However, if you create the coaching plan, it will be *your* coaching plan and not the client's, even if you are pulling the themes from your discussions. When clients develop their own goals they demonstrate higher performance against them than if someone else, like their organization or coach, sets them. In short, authorship of goals creates the ownership and energy to achieve them (Welsh, Baer, and Sessions 2020). Instead of falling into the trap of writing the plan for your client, facilitate the process in real time. We find we lose important momentum if we wait multiple sessions for a struggling client to complete the exercise on their own.

A final element of goal setting is asking them to consider the resources they can access for support. This may include questions such as:

- What strengths do you already have that will support you?
- Are there any role models that exemplify this goal for you?
- Who could help identify or provide access to upcoming development opportunities (e.g., projects, meetings…) that would provide a good "lab" as you practice new approaches?

SAMPLE COACHING PLANS

1. An excerpt from Claude's Coaching Plan

> Leadership Vision: I will become a leader who thinks, works, and communicates more strategically, increasing the value I deliver to the organization, and preparing myself for broader leadership roles.

GOALS (Changes to increase my effectiveness)	BEHAVIORS AND ACTIONS (Things to start or stop)	IMPACT OF ACHIEVING GOAL	SUCCESS MARKERS (How to know I'm making progress)
1. Connect with my audience with impact and efficiency	Take time to prepare: consider audience, write out key messages, prepare for likely questions Deliver the message: practice making clear, concise points; use pace and pauses to create dialogue; read the room and adjust accordingly	Greater influence on business decisions and strategic plans Reputation as a clear com-municator and valued collaborator	Peer and manager feedback Quick self-assessments after significant meetings and/or coach debriefs Invited to more meetings on critical topics
2. Create time for…			

2. An excerpt from Zuri's Coaching Plan

Overall Leadership Vision: Become a leader and colleague who approaches work and life with greater ease and a collaborative mindset to achieve more fulfillment and success with and through others.

BEHAVIORAL GOAL (3 max)	CHALLENGES TO THE GOAL	RESOURCES AVAILABLE	POTEN- TIAL ACTIONS	INTERNAL/ EXTERNAL SUCCESS MEASURES
1. Take more (calculated) risks	Fear of failure Feeling like an impostor	Track record of success Constant stream of requests/op- portunities Manager's encourage- ment	Develop courage mindset Chal- lenge more Ask more questions	Greater visibility More failures Greater confidence
2. Establish routines that support...				

Like any tool or framework, goal setting can be overused. Focusing solely on development goals risks your coaching slipping into a tactical, behavior-modification approach. A laser focus on goals can also narrow your coaching conversations, precluding important conversations about who the client is and the opportunity to deepen their self-awareness in a way that supports their overall development. It may feel counterintuitive, but a coaching plan that includes a leadership vision as well as meaning-ful goals creates the freedom to discuss emerging leadership issues the client is facing or to expand into different areas of development; the plan provides a home base to revisit, keeping the work on track.

SPONSOR ALIGNMENT ON THE COACHING GOALS AND PLAN

Once the client has done the work of integrating assessment results and their leadership vision, and developed their coaching goals and plan, it's time to bring the sponsor into the conversation to ensure align-ment with the organization. This alignment across the client, coach, and sponsor on goals and measures of success is essential to creating a successful coaching outcome (Burger and van Coller-Peter 2019). Typically the sponsor is the client's manager; sometimes an HR leader is involved. Following are the objectives of a sponsor alignment meeting:

- Ensure the organization is aware of and in agreement with the coaching goals and plan.
- The sponsor, client, and coach agree on what success looks like at the end of the engagement.
- The sponsor feels invested in the coaching and everyone is clear about how the sponsor can best support the client (e.g., offering feedback, touching base on how coaching is going, etc.).

Sometimes clients feel uncomfortable about the alignment meeting. Perhaps they feel vulnerable about sharing the assessment results or are uncomfortable asking their manager to focus on their develop-ment and not just business, or they simply may not understand the value of having the sponsor on board. We help them understand why it's an important part of the process and support them in feeling comfortable with it. To do this, we assure them of the confidential nature of the 1:1 coaching conversations. We also talk about the benefits of alignment:

- The client can be confident their coaching goals are in line with what the organization wants or needs from them.
- They are more likely to receive useful feedback from their sponsor that can help them calibrate and accelerate their development.
- They are building a foundation for ongoing development conversations with their sponsor.

The two key ingredients in productive sponsor alignment meetings are:

1. The client takes ownership of the content of the meeting and works with the coach to develop key messages and requests, and how they want to deliver them in the meeting.
2. The meeting focuses just enough on the look-back (assessment results) to give context, and more on the look-forward—the coaching goals, plan, and how everyone will support the client.

We coach clients to open the meeting by sharing their insights from the assessment results, whether or not they share the actual results. These insights include what the client learned from the assessments, what resonated with them, what surprised them, and if they need more clarity in certain areas. Then it's time to spend the bulk of the meeting discussing the client's goals and plan for coaching. Often this is a lively discussion for everyone. Our role is to support the client and sponsor by asking questions, offering perspectives, and helping clarify agreements.

TOP TIPS
KEEPING ALIGNMENT MEETINGS ON TRACK

- One way these meetings can go off track is if the client shifts into presentation mode instead of conversation mode. Even when discussed in advance, the client's potential discomfort may lead to a monologue and missed opportunity for input from the sponsor. As coach, you can help by encouraging pauses or stepping in to ask the sponsor a question.

- Another way these meetings can go off track is if the client or sponsor gets mired in detail or debate of the 360° feedback. If this happens, gently remind everyone of the importance of answering any high-level questions regarding the feedback, and focusing most of the attention on looking forward; i.e., the goals and plan.

- The sponsor may struggle to provide direct feedback or commit to their role. In this case, the coach or the client may need to ask a straightforward question to ensure alignment. For example, *"Are we aligned that these goals are what you believe are most important for Tom to be working on in coaching?"* Or, as the client requests ongoing support and feedback, we may ask a question to gain specificity. For example, if the sponsor has agreed to provide regular feedback, we may ask, *"When and how would that happen?"* to get to clear, constructive actions.

- Despite everyone's best intentions, sponsors and clients often fall short on their commitments to one another to regularly check in on the coaching. As the meeting wraps up, revisit what they've agreed to regarding sponsor-client feedback conversations, and what shape that will take. This gives you license later to check in about how those are going.

- In certain situations, such as a manager who has never sponsored coaching before, the coach, with the client's knowledge, may meet 1:1 with the sponsor to outline the purpose and roles of the alignment meeting, and in some cases, to offer guidance on how to best support the client in the conversation.

- If HR isn't formally involved in the sponsor alignment meeting, now is a great time to review what should be communicated with them about the engagement, depending on what expectations were set during contracting. You and your client may both need to take a step to share that you've hit a process milestone or to provide insight into the coaching goals. For example, you may connect with your HR contact and your client may connect with their HR business partner. Ensure agreement about what's being shared by whom, and then manage the process. It doesn't take much to attend to this, but it is easy to forget as the momentum for coaching builds.

The sponsor alignment meeting offers the coach additional insight into the dynamics between the client and sponsor, which can help the coach understand how best to support both the client and the sponsor during the engagement. Things we might pick up on include how directly they communicate, how engaged the sponsor seems, how well they understand and connect with one another, and the underlying emotional tenor of the interaction. These observations inform how we shape ongoing sponsor interactions.

Debriefing with the client following the alignment meeting is an opportunity to explore what the client thought went well and what they took away from it. It's also a time to discuss and capture adjustments the client wants to make to the plan and any next steps with the sponsor or others.

SETTING UP INFORMAL ALIGNMENT THROUGH STAKEHOLDER FEEDBACK

Once the client has aligned with the sponsor on the coaching goals, we explore the role of stakeholders. We encourage the client to engage in a direct, ongoing feedback loop with several stakeholders. The client may share one or more goals with each stakeholder and invite them to provide informal feedback throughout the coaching process—catching the client doing something well or noting when they are falling short of their goals. This ongoing feedback accelerates the client's growth because they get real-time readouts of the changes they're making.

In addition to providing feedback that supports the client's learning and shifts, when stakeholders are engaged in the coaching process, the client tends to become more effective (Goldsmith and Morgan 2004). It also helps the organization notice the progress, shortening the lag time between the client making a change and the organization perceiving it.

Often clients feel uncomfortable and vulnerable about asking stakeholders for feedback along the way, even when we've shared the benefit, namely of accelerating their development. It may be more amenable for the client to start slowly with just one or two stakeholders or to start later, a few months into the engagement.

CHAPTER 4 TAKEAWAYS

▶ Combining a visioning process with goal setting results in a compelling and energizing coaching plan that serves as a through line for your engagement.

▶ A well-crafted coaching plan provides the freedom to venture into new territory as your client gains self-awareness, as well as the space to discuss immediate leadership challenges.

▶ The coach may facilitate the process, but the client must author their vision, goals, and coaching plan.

▶ A robust coaching plan will include an overarching leadership vision or declaration, two or three specific goals with supporting behaviors and success measures, and be augmented by a discussion of potential challenges and resources.

▶ Completing this draft coaching plan signals that you and your client are ready to prepare for the organizational alignment meeting with the engagement sponsor.

▶ Organizational alignment is essential to a client's success; it ensures the organization is on board with the client's coaching plan and coaching goals and demonstrates commitment to coaching success in both directions.

▶ Early alignment with the sponsor provides a foundation for targeted ongoing feedback and future assessment of progress.

▶ Including stakeholders in the coaching journey benefits the client through encouraging constructive feedback about the changes they're making and helps the organization notice changes and alter perceptions.

PHASE III
MAKING PROGRESS

CREATING THE CONTAINER

ESTABLISHING THE THROUGH LINE

MAKING PROGRESS

ENDING WITH MEANING

5

Coaching
Sessions

CHAPTER 5

BEING INTENTIONAL: THE COACHING SESSION

I t was 1:55 and Andie was stressed. Her day had gone completely sideways. She'd scheduled plenty of time to catch up on her administrative tasks, but the day had other plans. Now she was five minutes out from a coaching session with Tom and she was scrambling, unable to even recall the highlights from their last meeting.

Andie opened her client notebook and started to review notes from their last session. Unfortunately, they were pretty scanty. Then she remembered she had scheduled another client right after Tom's last session, so she had not had time to clean up her notes and capture reflections. As she scanned the pages, she remembered that it had been a particularly intense conversation, and because she had been so immersed in it, she had just jotted down a few bullets and phrases. Now she was struggling to weave them together. She was edgy and annoyed with herself and only had three minutes to pull it together.

Recognizing that her head was not in a good place, Andie closed her notebook and took a deep breath. She closed her eyes and focused on centering, then asked herself how she wanted to show up for this meeting. She continued her breathing, slowing down her heart rate and grounding herself, then opened her eyes and opened her Zoom meeting room.

Then a text illuminated her phone. It was from another client who wanted to discuss an issue. She had another minute before her session with Tom. The rest of her day was nuts, and she knew that if she didn't respond now, she might not have a chance later on. She quickly looked at her schedule and texted her only available window to her client. They secured a time, and she sent an invite. Only then did she realize Tom had been waiting for a couple of minutes. Flustered, she quickly let him into the meeting room.

"I am so sorry to be late, Tom," she said in a rush. "I was a couple of minutes early and then got immersed in something, and before I knew it, it was 2:05!"

He smiled and said, "Not a problem, Andie; you've waited for me before!" But Andie still felt off; the centering she had done prior to receiving that text had evaporated. She tried to reground, but as she did, she missed what Tom was saying. Finally, she got into the groove and listened as Tom shared that he had been experimenting with new ways to engage his team and was making progress. The session flew by as she and Tom discussed what he was focused on as well as what he was planning moving forward.

As the session came to an end, Andie asked Tom how things were going with Sydney. "Good," he said. Sydney liked his coaching plan, which the three of them had discussed in their sponsor alignment meeting, even making some suggestions for how he might experiment with delegation. "She seems more connected to what I'm working on now," Tom said. "She pulled me aside after a team meeting Monday and said it was clear that I had been focused on leveraging my team more and that they were stepping up to meet the challenge."

"That's terrific, Tom!" Andie said. "It's great that Sydney is more connected to your development. Have a good couple of weeks, and I'll look forward to our next meeting." And with that, the session concluded.

Andie stood and took a deep breath. She had another meeting in ten minutes and she knew she should be prepping for it, but she needed to clear her head. She walked to the window and reflected on the session with Tom. It had gone OK, but she felt like she had been in consultant mode more than coach mode, which she knew could happen when she was feeling overextended and less present. The stressful run-up to the meeting was still on her mind, as well as her messy pre-session preparation. This was becoming a pattern; she was trying to do too much in too little time.

○ ○ ○

We now turn our attention to the processes and practices we use before, during, and after coaching sessions. These are key aspects of intentional engagement and essential to **Making Progress**, the third phase of the framework. There are five elements that require attention and thought.

THE COACHING SESSION: KEY ELEMENTS

* Capacity and scheduling
* Pre-session preparation
* The coaching session
* Post-session documentation
* Post-session reflection

CAPACITY AND SCHEDULING

To do our best coaching, we need time to prepare for a session, and that begins with client capacity and scheduling.

Many newer coaches have asked us what is the "right" number of clients to work with at any given time. Unfortunately, there is no magic number. Determining that number for you depends on several factors. For example:

- How many hours do you want to work?
- How much do you want to earn from coaching?
- Are you seeing your clients virtually or in person?
- If you are seeing your clients in person, what is the travel time required?
- Do you typically see your clients once a month, twice a month, or more frequently?
- How long is a typical session? A typical engagement?
- Do you spend time doing other work in addition to coaching?

An additional factor to consider that affects client load is managing client starts. You may have capacity for a certain number of clients, but it would be incredibly difficult to start them all at once because the first two months of a client engagement are typically more time-intensive due to client intake, kickoff, and assessment activities.

Through the years, we have experimented with managing our coaching capacity and have learned to pay less attention to the number of clients and more attention to the conditions we need to do our best coaching. The question we invite you to contemplate is "What is the right number of clients for me to have a meaningful and sustainable coaching practice?"

This shifts our attention to a different set of criteria:

1. Do I have the time to schedule clients with windows for both pre-session preparation and post-session reflection and documentation?
2. Do I have the capacity to be truly present with each client?
3. Have I factored in time for running my practice (e.g., business development, writing proposals, invoicing)?
4. Have I factored in time for ongoing professional development?
5. Am I clear on the work-life balance I am trying to strike and honoring that intention?

Then there is the unfortunate reality that clients do not materialize on our timeline, so there will be periods when we feel we have too many clients or too few. Similarly, clients' schedules won't always align with our plans and structures; scheduling clients back-to-back may be unavoidable at times. Our experience is that there is rarely a perfect balance, but paying attention to these dynamics gives us the ability to evaluate the trade-offs and make intentional choices.

During our interviews, many coaches shared that they constantly monitor their capacity and how it matches their intentions. For coaches employed by coaching firms and for internal coaches, the challenge is different but equally compelling. How do you meet the expectations of your employer while ensuring you have the time you need to coach at your best?

Making Space

There was a period of time during Joe's coaching career when he was juggling way too many client commitments. He was significantly over-extended but was managing to keep all the balls in the air, in no small part because he had a terrific memory for details and events. During this time, he would often hurry from one coaching client to the next, never late but always feeling on the verge. He took notes in coaching sessions, but other than a quick glance before starting a session rarely referred to them. After all, his memory got him through every time.

The pace he was keeping limited the time he had to prepare for client sessions to a minute or two of breathing and reflection, and this was often lost to his need to return emails or phone calls. The same was true for reflection after sessions. When he looks back on that time, Joe is embarrassed by the truth—that his ego was fueled by the great clients he had and the progress they made. It was a rush!

Despite the good results and happy clients, at times Joe felt a disconnect. For the most part, his clients were thrilled with the coaching, but he knew in his heart that he could be doing a better job. He knew that if he slowed down and attended to the time before and after each session, he would be more present and better able to support his clients. So he made a conscious decision to do just that. He right-sized his practice so that he would have the time he needed to attend to each client, and he has since felt more fulfilled by and deeply connected to his work.

There are as many approaches to scheduling as there are coaches. Some coaches offer set days and hours to their clients while others schedule based on mutual availability. We know some coaches who use virtual assistants or scheduling software to manage their client appointments, while others feel giving over control of their schedule would be unthinkable.

We asked our coaching colleagues how they manage their calendars. We share their examples here to spark ideas for your own experimentation:

- Liz initially made herself available whenever clients wanted and realized quickly that it didn't work for her. Now she schedules with clients Tuesday through Thursday, saving Monday and Friday for managing her practice and professional development activities.
- Jose schedules clients during the second and fourth weeks of the month, and uses the first and third weeks for projects, business development, professional development, and practice management.
- Ben arranges standing meetings for the duration of coaching, based on the cadence and day of the week that works well for the client; they adjust as needed.
- Stacy offers her clients windows in the evening and on weekends because the majority of her clients cannot be available during typical working hours.
- Jason schedules clients Monday through Friday and works to be available when his clients need him. He takes advantage of downtime that naturally occurs around his client needs to attend to admin work and professional development.
- Jess uses Calendly for 360° participant interviews. For client meetings, she schedules the next session directly with the client at the end of each meeting.
- Veronica uses a virtual assistant for much of her scheduling, especially for 360° interviews and with clients who have EAs who handle their schedule.

> **Capacity Creep**
>
> *A couple of years ago Dani's husband Sam told her, "You know, you once told me that one of the reasons you have your own coaching practice is so that if you want to take yoga at 10 a.m. on a Wednesday, you can. Except I never see you taking yoga at 10 a.m. EVER." That brief conversation made a huge impact, and she began managing her calendar to provide more balance, blocking out times every week for activities like yoga. She also began blocking windows during the week for administrative work that almost always ended up taking time on the weekends.*

If you are trying to land on the best approach, we encourage you to experiment. As a first step, take the time to consider what you need to do your best coaching. Once you understand this, you are in a better position to schedule intentionally and to navigate the times when demand is too high or too low.

PRE-SESSION PREPARATION

PREPARING YOURSELF

There are two elements of pre-session preparation: *content and process review*, which is focused on reviewing recent notes and reflecting on the arc of the engagement, and *internal preparation to center and manage your presence*. In this chapter we will focus on content and process preparation; we'll dive into the topic of centering and managing presence in Chapter 8.

Focusing on content and process can sound bigger than it actually is. In practice, it consists of reviewing notes from your last sessions and considering what will serve the client best in their upcoming session. This can take just a few minutes or may extend longer depending on the phase of the coaching engagement. For example, if you are going to debrief assessments with your client, you will probably review the assessment reports and consider how to best engage with them as they receive their feedback. If you're well into the coaching, you may quickly review the last session's notes and reflections. And if you're nearing the end of the engagement, you might review your reflections from across the engagement to remind yourself of key themes and the distance the client has traveled. While we believe in the value of preparation, it is important to maintain perspective. Be *informed by your preparation but not anchored to it,* as a client may arrive at a session with an unexpected need to go in a different direction.

Prep & Flex

Brooke was coaching Steve, a senior leader at a SAS company. The engagement was focused on CEO succession, and Steve's coaching was part of his candidacy for the CEO role. Brooke had spent the past month immersed in Steve's assessments: conducting interviews, working with an online assessment tool the client requested, and writing up the results of everything. After a month of intense activity and preparation, she was ready and excited to share the work and insights with him.

Arriving at Steve's office, Brooke said hello and took a seat, asking him how he was but really just thinking about launching into sharing the assessment results she had labored over. At which point Steve shared that he had suffered a cardiac episode two weeks prior, and no one knew about it at work. At that moment, time stood still. Brooke took a deep breath and put the assessments aside, literally AND figuratively. They spent the next two hours discussing what had happened and how it could change his future. They did return to the assessment results, but not until the following month and after he had decided to withdraw from consideration as the CEO. The assessment information was still important and useful to their work together, as Steve remained in a significant leadership position, but they were now looking at it through a different lens.

PRE-SESSION CLIENT PREPARATION

A different aspect of preparation focuses on preparing your client for the session. While writing this book, we spoke with many coaches who do not prepare their clients before a session, and just as many who do.

Coaches who do *not* have a regular client preparation process share the philosophy that coaching is a client-driven experience, and that pre-session preparation for clients is "doing the work the client needs to own." Another factor that contributes to some coaches selecting this approach is the concern that a client might cancel a coaching conversation simply because they've not done the "homework."

Coaches who *do* have a regular client preparation process believe that the process results in clients who show up well prepared, leading to more substantial coaching conversations. These coaches use a continuum of approaches, ranging from sending a brief email containing a few reflective questions for the client to consider, to sending a pre-session prep form the client fills out and returns to the coach prior to each meeting.

We both do some form of client preparation before a session. Our approaches differ, but they both fall in the center of the continuum described above. Typically, we email our clients with a few reflective questions prior to their session. We have some consistent questions that we customize when useful. However, neither of us requires our clients to send us responses prior to the meeting. We find this to be a nice balance of encouraging client reflection ahead of meetings while allowing the client to hold themselves accountable for making the most of each conversation.

If you are interested in adding pre-session client preparation to your approach, we encourage you to experiment and ask your client what works for them. You may even find yourself varying your approach over the course of the engagement based on client feedback.

SAMPLE CLIENT PREP EMAIL

Hi Ivan,

Hope you've had a great weekend. I'm looking forward to seeing you tomorrow. I'll text you when I get to the office and have made my way through security in the lobby.

Ahead of our conversation, here are a few questions to think about as a way of helping us shape our time together:

1. How are you living into your leadership vision?
2. What progress are you making on your coaching plan? What challenges or roadblocks are you running into?
3. What's most on your mind that we should explore in this coaching conversation?

No need to send written responses unless that's helpful for you. See you soon.

Warmly,
Max

THE COACHING SESSION

BEGINNING THE SESSION

Coaching conversations that meander, get stuck, feel flat, or somehow seem less than great can often be traced back to skipping or poorly executing the *session contracting* discussion. As we discussed in Chapter 1, session contracting is used early in a session to surface what is foremost on the client's mind and what they want to accomplish during the session. Session contracting is simple, but is easy to skip, especially if the client shows up in a state of high emotion or a strong drive to action. We cannot stress enough the importance of aligning with your client early in each coaching session to ensure you are on the same page about what to explore together during the session. A consistent session contracting conversation at the start of every session builds a shared understanding that your sessions will focus on the coaching plan you have developed, while also making time to discuss situations that surface on the spot.

DURING THE SESSION

Note-taking during coaching sessions is highly coach specific. We know coaches who take copious notes during the session, those who capture key words and phrases, others who create mind maps, and still others who do not take notes at all. Some swear by typing notes while others insist on handwriting them. Regardless of their approach, all agree that consistently focusing on a notebook or a screen containing your notes breaks your connection with your client and should be avoided.

We tapped into our network again to offer meaningful examples of how other coaches take notes. Use these to spark ideas for your own experimentation:

- Sophie takes copious handwritten notes and reviews them prior to the next session.
- Scott does not take notes at all but saves fifteen minutes after the session to write down what was most significant about the conversation.

- Jess types notes when meeting with clients by phone and handwritten notes when in person as she finds the computer a barrier in these situations.
- Bob captures words and phrases throughout the session and then uses them to document key themes and takeaways after the session.
- Cari uses a shared Google doc with her client where she captures a few bullets as well as homework and next steps.
- Kate notes key ideas as a reminder to come back to a topic. She also captures hypotheses or feelings she has throughout the session.

There is no one-size-fits-all answer when it comes to note-taking. However, consider that whatever approach you use, it should enable you to be fully present and engaged with your client. You may wish to look back at some of your client notes, consider how you are using them, and perhaps be inspired to experiment with a different approach.

CONCLUDING THE SESSION

Many of us have had coaching sessions where the conversation was so rich and impactful that we did not want to abruptly shift gears to end the session. But how you conclude a session affects how your client integrates and applies the work you have done together. This is due in part to the recency effect—that individuals are more likely to retain information discussed at the end of a conversation.

We end our coaching sessions with a consistent closing practice, which provides the client time to briefly reflect, build awareness, and gather insights on what was most significant from the session.

Our process is simple: We ask the client to share their insights from the session and what they would like us to follow up on in the next session. This is an easy way to learn from the client what is most on their mind, and it creates a sense of continuity and accountability. It is also useful to understand what our *client* finds most impactful and how that aligns with what *we* thought was most impactful.

Clients will typically share one to three headlines, and we capture these as bullets in a box at the end of our notes. The clear delineation of bullets in a box begins our post-session documentation process. This practice creates a thread from session to session, as we can check in on these takeaways and follow-up items at the start of the next session.

Building a regular closing practice creates a shared expectation that this is how you will end the session, which supports a smoother and more consistent conclusion to each session. You might even find that clients start to anticipate this wrap-up practice and drive toward it themselves as coaching meetings approach the end time.

POST-SESSION DOCUMENTATION

We use the term post-session documentation to denote the process of reviewing your session notes, highlighting key themes, and adding comments to augment what was captured in the session. Spending a few minutes on this after a coaching session ensures that you will have a clear set of notes and insights to facilitate preparation for your next session, as well as a record of any steps you want to take before the next meeting. While it is not necessary to do this immediately following a session, the more time that elapses, the harder it will be to make sense of your notes, particularly if you are only capturing key phrases.

Notably, there is a growing trend for coaches to send their clients highlights summarizing the coaching session. Similar to client preparation, coaches are divided into two schools of thought: those who find that post-session highlights support the client's ability to reflect and prepare for the next session and those who believe it is the client's responsibility to capture their insights along the way. We fall into the latter camp and do not send our clients session summaries—although on occasion we will send a follow-up email with an article or tool we discussed in session or a follow-up question if the client has requested this support.

POST-SESSION REFLECTION

While related, post-session reflection is different from documentation. When done well, these processes dovetail and support each other. Post-session reflection is the term we use for intentionally pausing and considering the coaching session you just concluded. It invites you to step back and look at the coaching relationship, yourself as coach, and the work you are doing with the client. By removing that immediacy and looking at the session as an observer rather than a participant, you are able to view the situation from the outside in. Robert Kegan describes this as the subject-object relationship. When you are immersed in an experience, you are subject to it, and it is challenging to see all aspects of the experience clearly. Reflecting on and examining a past experience without being embedded in it creates the opportunity to consider the experience with greater objectivity, to harvest insights, and to integrate learnings (Kegan 1994). Why is this important to coaches?

Imagine you are swimming laps. You feel the water on your skin as you propel yourself forward, you feel your arms and legs working in perfect sync, you can hear your heart beating, and you can see the wall of the pool as you approach it. It is a powerful immersive experience, but in that moment, it might be hard to see if you are swimming in a straight line. Now imagine yourself on the side of the pool, watching yourself swim. With this perspective, you can see things more objectively and notice things you were unable to see when you were immersed in the moment. For example, you are now able to see that you aren't swimming in a straight line and that it is because you are stroking harder with your left arm. This awareness enables you to make a change.

Creating time to reflect on your coaching sessions is the act of putting yourself on the side of the pool. Taking the time to reflect and capture insights about our client, the session, and ourselves as coaches enhances our ability to look at the session objectively and gather valuable insights and lessons that would otherwise escape us. We are more likely to identify issues and opportunities while reflecting than we would if we rely solely on our experience in the session.

As coaches, it is critical that we are able to understand our own developmental edges and shadows. Bob Anderson, creator of The Leadership Circle Profile, offers, "That which we do not see drives us." In other words, if we are unaware of our own need for approval or drive for results, we risk that shadow driving how we coach. Being able to surface and understand our shadows enables us to work through them and build the capacity to coach from a place of greater consciousness.

Your reflection practice may be as simple as contemplating "What went well and what might I do differently next time?" Or you may choose to focus your reflection on a shadow or learning edge that you are working on, such as deepening your presence or managing boundaries. We explore learning edges and development further in Chapter 9.

If you are short on time or find it difficult to build a consistent reflective practice, you might try this simple but effective technique. Following a coaching session, ask yourself three questions and jot short responses in the margin of your meeting notes or on a Post-it note, then include those responses in the notes for the session. The questions may be as simple as:

- What went well in the session? Why?
- What would I do differently if I had a "do-over"?
- What are potential next steps to explore?

Using this technique gives you access to the experience of the session and opens the door for further reflection. For example, if you notice that the session felt unfocused, later you might ask yourself why. Did you begin without session contracting? Are you missing alignment on coaching goals? You will harvest insights immediately and can revisit the reflections as you return to the notes to prepare for the next session.

Post-its for Deep Reflection

Lee was introduced to a reflective technique by her good friend and colleague, Deb Gerardi. The goal was for Lee to observe her coaching from a Self as Coach perspective. She chose small Post-its of different colors and reflected on these questions after each coaching conversation:

- *What was my energy like before and after the session? (Pink Post-it)*
- *What emotions came up for me during the session? (Blue Post-it)*
- *What hunches did I have during the session and now? (Yellow Post-it)*

The color-coded Post-its allowed real-time capture, then later reflection within the coaching engagement and across different coaching engagements. For example, if energy shifted during the session, she'd ask herself why. Was this a pattern with this client? With other clients? What emotions surfaced, and are they related to energy? Are they useful if my client and I look at them as a proxy for the experience others have when engaging with my client? How am I using the hunches and what do they mean for how I'm working with clients?

Another way to build your reflective practice is to work with a coaching supervisor. During a coaching supervision session, a coach partners with a certified supervisor to focus on their ongoing development, often by reflecting on current coaching cases. Coaching supervision either 1:1 or in a small group setting is effective for personal and professional development (Downing 2021). We discuss coaching supervision further in Chapter 9.

○ ○ ○

CHAPTER 5 TAKEAWAYS

▶ Preparation allows coaches to enter a coaching session focused on the client and fully engaged in their development. And remember to be informed but not anchored to your preparation.

▶ Each coach needs to find a comfortable and effective approach to document relevant information during a session while still maintaining a connection with the client.

▶ Using a simple but intentional closing practice can increase the impact of a session for the client and create a connection from session to session.

▶ Spending a short, focused period of time on documentation after a coaching session creates a clear set of notes to facilitate preparation for the next session.

▶ Building a consistent reflective practice increases a coach's awareness and capabilities as a coach.

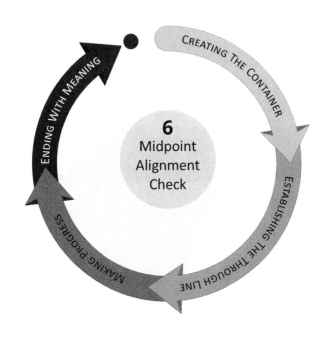

CREATING THE CONTAINER

ESTABLISHING THE THROUGH LINE

MAKING PROGRESS

ENDING WITH MEANING

6
Midpoint
Alignment
Check

CHAPTER 6

PAUSING TO CHECK CONNECTION: MID-ENGAGEMENT ALIGNMENT

W alking in the park midday with her dog Charlie was an important ritual for Andie. It got her up and out of her office and into the world and often provided quiet time to reflect and prepare for a client session. Switching off the podcast she was listening to, she shifted her attention to her upcoming meeting with Tom, which was also their mid-engagement check-in.

Mid-engagement check-ins made Andie a little uncomfortable. It was easy to help her clients focus on the work they had done to date, but she found it awkward to ask clients for feedback. She persisted, though, knowing how important the process was to a successful engagement.

Last week she had a mid-engagement check-in with a different client, Melinda, and it had yielded some great insights. Melinda was a client who appreciated time to prepare and always used pre-session reflection questions to get ready for their session. Knowing this, Andie provided her with specific midpoint questions ahead of time. Melinda had been thoughtful in her reflections, and they had a great conversation, noticing her progress as well as places that had been less successful and required pivots. Melinda particularly loved the prep question "What would taking it up a notch look, sound, and feel like?" She shared that now that she'd established a better time management approach and was feeling more in control of her schedule, she really wanted to dive in to ruthless prioritization to create more time for reflection and strategic thinking. Melinda also provided some useful feedback for Andie; she confirmed that their relationship was strong and suggested that it could be further strengthened and successful if Andie challenged her more often and deeply when Melinda wasn't making time for strategic reflection. They discussed specifically what that would entail and agreed to try this together.

Tom was different. He did not like pre-work, saying it stressed him out, so Andie would take a different approach with him. She mentally carved out a few minutes of the mid-engagement session discussion for Tom to pause and reflect on the mid-engagement questions before they started the discussion. She knew this would help him harvest the wins and feedback he had received and consider what they could do differently together to make the balance of their engagement even more successful.

Intentions set, she pulled a bright orange ball out of her pocket and then watched as Charlie made a mad dash for the ball as it flew through the air.

○ ○ ○

Adding a structured check-in point with your client several months into the engagement serves several purposes: assessing progress on goals, strengthening the coach-client relationship, and optimizing the coaching approach. It also serves as a preparation for a sponsor mid-engagement meeting, should that be part of the coaching engagement. These midpoint alignment check-in points are another important component of **Making Progress**; they can affirm and motivate clients and may also surface challenges that still need to be addressed.

MID-ENGAGEMENT ALIGNMENT: KEY ELEMENTS

- Informal approaches to aligning with your client
- Structured coach-client mid-engagement review
- Optional sponsor mid-engagement meeting

INFORMAL APPROACHES

There are many ways to stay connected to and aligned with your client over the normal course of a coaching engagement. Most coaches we know rely on one or more of the following:

Session contracting. Contracting for each conversation, taking the time to agree on how to use the time you have together, and revisiting the contract at the end of the conversation to ensure you covered everything keeps you and the client aligned.

Naming progress and tying it back to the coaching plan. In coaching conversations, especially when the client is updating us or telling a story, we may hear successes related to a goal, and if the client doesn't name it as such, we'll acknowledge the progress and tie it back to a goal. We may also see patterns of success over multiple conversations and name those for the client as well. Ahead of certain coaching conversations, we may ask clients to review their coaching plan and come prepared to share successes and challenges.

Asking for what the client wants. Asking the client what support they would like from the coach during or between conversations helps identify ways of working together that the coach may not come up with on their own.

As part of your regular reflection, we encourage you to ask yourself: When was the last time my client and I referenced their leadership vision and coaching plan? When did I last ask my client what they'd like from me, or how they're experiencing the coaching? This helps build a habit around staying aligned with your client.

STRUCTURED COACH-CLIENT MID-ENGAGEMENT REVIEW

By the time we're a few months into the engagement and a rhythm has been established, it's tempting to stay in that rhythm and not deliberately pause to check in with the client about their progress, the client-coach relationship, and the process of coaching. We might also avoid a more structured check-in because we aren't sensing the client has made progress they want to recognize, or any number of other reasons. But coaching is a dynamic process, so relying on your initial coach-client contracting discussion in your kickoff meeting freezes that discussion at an early point in time, missing opportunities to evolve and strengthen your coaching alliance (Pliopas 2021). So, while it may feel tempting to skip, we prioritize this discussion. Every time we have this conversation with our clients, we learn something that leads to even better outcomes.

Both the client and the coach benefit from pausing the activity of coaching to reflect on where they've been and where they're heading. Clients pause to take inventory, celebrate successes, and recommit to development. They also get to practice offering feedback and making requests in a safe, supportive relationship; this further strengthens the working alliance and can accelerate progress (Anseel et al. 2015). Coaches are able to role model how to receive, explore, and respond to feedback and benefit by becoming aware of opportunities to work more effectively with their client.

We remind our clients that we will have a midpoint check-in in the prior session. Depending on the client and their desire or lack of desire for preparation, we may share a set of reflection questions for them to complete ahead of time. The topics we ask them to reflect on include:

Coaching goals. progress, challenges, and possible shifts in goals

Coaching relationship and approach. what's working well in the coaching; what could be improved; how the client and coach can better support where the client wants to go in their coaching work

Clients can feel awkward talking about the coaching relationship and process or may feel uncomfortable about sharing constructive feedback. It's helpful to frame this as an opportunity for them to practice offering feedback, asking for what they need, and being intentional about an important work relationship—all things they can bring into other work relationships.

Tweaking a Habitual Approach

As part of her standard coaching approach, Jani sends a prep email to her clients with reflection questions ahead of a scheduled call. When she and David had their coach-client mid-engagement review, David shared that the questions created stress given how busy he was and how seriously he wanted to take the coaching work. He often worked past midnight the night before coaching to craft well-articulated, thoughtful responses, and as a result didn't feel it was his best work in preparing or showing up for the coaching conversations. Together Jani and David explored what would better serve David and agreed on a different approach: sharing questions after each conversation. This better suited David's personal reflection process, which was fired up by the coaching conversations. Jani was grateful to have learned this about David and now regularly asks clients about their preparation and reflection preferences in their kickoff meeting.

Most often, we incorporate a mid-engagement check-in into a scheduled coaching conversation. We ask the client if they would prefer to take the first 20 to 30 minutes for it or the last, and then move into a coaching conversation guided by the client's agenda. We've also had the conversation as a stand-alone meeting, which is useful especially if, in addition to the coach-client check-in, you and the client are also preparing for a mid-engagement sponsor meeting.

OPTIONAL MID-ENGAGEMENT SPONSOR MEETING: ALIGNING ON PROGRESS AND REVISITING THE COACHING PLAN

When coaching engagements are scoped for six months, a sponsor mid-engagement meeting is optional and depends on the contract and the client situation. This is because you probably met with your client and sponsor six to eight weeks into the engagement to review and gain alignment on the client's coaching plan. A mid-engagement meeting one month after that can feel like too much. When engagements are longer than six months, plan to have a mid-engagement sponsor meeting to continue building sponsor alignment and support for your client.

This sponsor meeting helps increase support for the coaching goals and the progress. It's useful to do this after several months of coaching and when the client is experiencing successes such as increased self-awareness, changes in behavior, or a growing skill/capability. Other reasons to conduct a mid-engagement sponsor meeting:

- The client and organization are seeking changes that are time-sensitive
- The sponsor isn't able to be as engaged or notice changes and offer feedback as expected

- The client's responsibilities or the organizational structure has changed; or
- There has been a change in the client's sponsor

A mid-engagement meeting is an opportunity for the client to share their reflections about the successes and challenges of each goal, hear feedback from the sponsor, and discuss any shifts in goals that may be necessary. It creates a checkpoint for the organization and the client to assess progress and determine where to focus efforts for the rest of the engagement. This meeting can also motivate the client for the continued effort that coaching requires.

In certain circumstances you may elect to have a pre-meeting with the sponsor to share the meeting objectives and to provide the sponsor with some light coaching on how they can best support the client during the meeting.

Sponsor on the Sidelines

Phil had a client whose boss did not want to be involved in the coaching engagement. He was standing on the sidelines and went so far as to tell Phil, "Let me know when it's over and if you need anything." When Phil asked about checking in at the midpoint of the engagement, the client's boss said, "No ... I'm busy, just do the work." But then, at the end of the engagement he said, "I saw some change but not very much ... this could have been better."

It was a true wake-up call for Phil. Now if he is not getting sponsor engagement, he raises the flag and says, "We need a checkpoint." And if he doesn't get a response, he will pause the engagement until he does.

These prep questions can be used to support the coach-client mid-engagement session and the optional sponsor mid-engagement. We find it useful to include questions about the overall engagement as well as each specific goal.

- What are your most important learnings so far?
- How are you moving toward your leadership vision?
- What are you most proud of so far?
- Where do you want to focus as you continue?
- What is working well in the coaching process? What, if anything, should we adjust in our process?

Mid-engagement alignment can take different forms depending on the duration of the engagement, the speed of client progress, and the engagement contract. At a minimum, support your client to reflect on their progress to date, make any needed adjustments to the coaching goals and the coaching process/interactions, and consider whether any organizational alignment is needed at this point.

CHAPTER 6 TAKEAWAYS

- ▶ Alignment happens through informal, ongoing interactions and more structured ones; coaches should attend to both.
- ▶ A client mid-engagement check-in benefits the client and the coach and can accelerate the client's progress in a meaningful way. It's easy to skip this step, but don't.
- ▶ An optional mid-engagement sponsor meeting ensures alignment and ongoing commitment in both directions, allows for midcourse correction, and generates momentum and clarity moving into the next phase of coaching.

PHASE IV

ENDING WITH MEANING

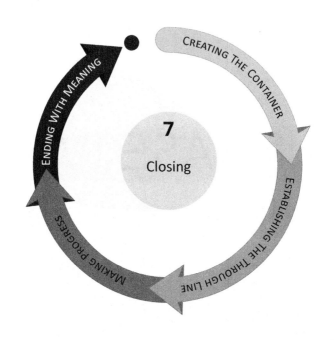

CHAPTER 7

FINISHING STRONG:
CLOSING A COACHING ENGAGEMENT

A ndie grabbed her bag and water and walked out of her yoga studio feeling recharged. The class had been good for her. She had been out of sorts all day and just couldn't shake it off. Probably because of all the transitions in process.

Starting new clients was so much work: creating the SOW, kickoff, intake, and conducting assessments. But today she was also thinking about her two clients who were wrapping up their engagements. She hated endings. Well, not every ending—on occasion there was a client she was glad to finish. One of these, Robert, was wrapping up tomorrow. While they had made significant progress, that engagement had been a lot of work from the start, and Andie was ready for it to end.

She was also starting to close her engagement with Tom, which would be bittersweet, but it was beyond time. It had been hard to pin Tom down over the past month as he had rescheduled a couple of times. He had done such great work that she did not think he was avoiding her; instead she had begun to suspect that he did not want the engagement to end. She played a role in the delay too as she had not been tracking their time that closely, and by the time she realized what was happening, they were well beyond the end date of their engagement.

When they finally did connect, Andie asked him what was going on and he confirmed her suspicions, admitting that he was not ready for their work together to come to an end. This initiated a good talk about transitions, and Andie reminded him that she would always be available by email, and they already had a 10,000-mile tune-up session scheduled two months after the end of their engagement.

In preparation for the close, Andie had done a progress assessment, conducting brief follow-up interviews with five participants from his initial 360° assessment. Overall, they shared that Tom had made significant shifts. There were still a few things that they noted as ongoing opportunities, but this was normal and actually signaled that people were being thoughtful and candid in their feedback. Those opportunities would be a part of Tom's Ongoing Development Plan. It had been fun to share the feedback with Tom and see how pleased he was that his hard work had been noticed.

This week they would meet to discuss the Ongoing Development Plan, and later in the month they would have a closing meeting with Sydney—another lag, as it had been hard to find a time that worked for the three of them.

Finally, the time for Tom's last coaching session arrived. Together they reflected on the meeting with Sydney. While she would never be accused of being an overinvolved leader, Sydney had stepped up to support Tom's coaching by giving him constructive feedback in their biweekly 1:1 meetings. She also gave him real-time feedback when she noticed something going well. Then Andie shifted the discussion to reflecting on the past six-plus months, briefly reviewing Tom's Ongoing Development Plan, and discussing what lay ahead for him.

As the time drew to a close, Andie said, "Tom, it's been such a pleasure and honor to work with you over the past six months. I'm happy you feel good about the progress you've made and the hard work you've invested in yourself."

Tom laughed. "Six months? More like eight by the time you wrangled me and Sydney! I really appreciate you putting up with us."

Andie smiled. "Well, we got here, and that's what's most important. I'll look forward to reconnecting with you for the 10,000-mile tune-up meeting in a couple of months, and in the interim I'm always an email or a phone call away if I can be helpful."

"Thank you, Andie," Tom said. "This has been a terrific experience. I can't say it was always fun or easy, but you supported me every step of the way. Just the fact that I look forward to my team meetings now instead of dreading them is huge. I'm so glad we have the 10,000-mile tune-up on the calendar and really appreciate your offer to connect if something comes up beforehand. I'll take you up on it if I need to!"

And with that, they said good-bye and signed off.

○ ○ ○

Endings can be full of emotion and sometimes even resistance, for your client and perhaps for you. When you tell the client that you're nearing the finish, they may think or say aloud, "Wait, what? We're at the end? But I'm not ready yet!" In the last phase, **Ending With Meaning**, we review and celebrate the progress made and create a plan to sustain the progress. Being intentional about these things ensures that the closing of an engagement is as impactful as the work that preceded it.

Given the human tendency to avoid endings or good-byes, at this point in the coaching we're on the lookout for subtle resistance around ending, such as the client stretching the time between sessions. We want to stay on top of the work so we can cross the finish line strong and set up the client for sustained success.

When is it time to wrap up? Here are a few signs:

1. The client has achieved their goals.
2. The client starts coaching themselves in your conversations: Client: "So today I want to talk about how I handled the board presentation last week. And I know you're going to ask me what I did well, so I'll start there. See, I'm learning!"
3. The contract is time-bound, and we've reached the time to end.

While wrapping up means an end to the engagement, it doesn't mean an end to the client's leadership vision, the learnings/practices/skills they acquired, or the relationship between coach and client.

CLOSING A COACHING ENGAGEMENT: KEY ELEMENTS

- Finishing strong
- Preparing the client for the closing
- Using progress feedback
- Final reflections and Ongoing Development Plan
- The final sponsor meeting
- Closing with the client and with yourself

FINISHING STRONG

We've all had at least a few client engagements where the closing feels more like a weak, drawn-out whimper rather than an exclamation point punctuating the end of a great engagement. What gets in the way of a strong wrap-up? Potential watch-outs include:

1. The client keeps bringing new things to work on in coaching, so the work doesn't feel finished.

2. The energy for coaching has fizzled out, and the client and sponsor don't seem interested in a proper wrap-up.

3. The sponsor wrap-up meeting gets delayed until weeks or even months after coaching conversations have ended.

4. The client or sponsor shares privately that they don't feel they've made progress.

5. The time stretches between meetings, affecting energy and momentum.

6. You're really enjoying the client and the coaching work, so you let it trail on ... and on ...

A strong conclusion encourages the client to fully reflect on and harvest their learnings. It allows for celebration of the hard work and success, and it sets the client up for sustained progress. Additionally, a strong conclusion involves the sponsor; as Julie Starr reminds us, "great coaching plus poor communication equals poor perception." Sponsor involvement at the end helps the organization notice changes, shift perceptions, and understand how to reinforce the client's growth.

Like other processes and tools we've shared here, concluding an engagement takes different forms based on what best supports the client and the organization. Following are some of the elements that create the conditions for a strong ending:

- Discussing and agreeing at the outset about how the engagement will end leads to a more satisfying conclusion (Cox 2010)
- Client reflection on their development journey
- Co-creation of an ongoing development plan to sustain progress and plan for future growth
- Sharing learnings and the plan with the sponsor
- Honoring the journey and celebrating success
- A concluding meeting for the client and coach following the sponsor wrap-up meeting

PREPARING THE CLIENT FOR CLOSING

A couple of sessions before the end of the engagement, we raise the topic of wrapping up. This helps create a sense of timing, clarifies the most important things to focus on in the last coaching conversations, and mentally prepares the client for finishing the coaching. Clients may react with a range of emotions: excitement, surprise, sadness, relief, worry or pride. The early signal of "Ending Ahead" provides an opportunity to recognize and work through these emotions as you near completion. When we tee up the conversation about wrap-up, we intentionally frame it as a successful end to a coaching engagement, pointing to the hard work they have invested and celebrating the progress they have made.

What we explore with the client at this point:

What is involved. Reflection and planning; possible feedback collection; coach-client meetings, and sponsor wrap-up meeting

Outcomes. Why closing with intention is important and what the client would like to take from it.

Timing. The timing for completing the engagement and deciding when to schedule the sponsor wrap-up meeting.

During this conversation we co-create a road map for completion that outlines the balance of the coaching.

Watch Out for Calendar Slide!

Callie was enjoying working with Ted, a recently promoted CMO in a start-up. So much so that she was allowing calendar slide; at the four-month mark of a six-month engagement, Ted requested they stretch their remaining sessions into the seventh or eighth month to accommodate an important project. Callie agreed.

When they tried to schedule the sponsor wrap-up with the CEO, it ultimately landed on the calendar in month ten. In the interim, the CMO got a new manager, who would now serve as sponsor. During the wrap-up meeting with the CEO and CMO, the new sponsor persisted in viewing the original coaching plan through the lens of the business's current challenges, not those of ten months ago. The sponsor wrap-up felt off the mark and didn't allow the client or the organization to celebrate the hard work and accomplishment against the coaching goals, nor did it set up the client for success against emerging, higher-stakes performance goals demanded by the new environment. The coaching work, which had energy and great outcomes through month four, was, understandably, judged by different goalposts at month ten. Callie wished she'd handled the request to stretch out the work and the wrap-up meeting differently. These days she's careful not to be overly accommodating to these requests.

USING PROGRESS FEEDBACK

Progress feedback offers insight about the changes the organization has noticed and should celebrate, as well as useful pointers about where to focus ongoing efforts. Additionally, collecting feedback reminds stakeholders of the client's goals and effort, and helps shift organizational perception faster than if feedback were not collected. In short, just asking about progress helps people notice the improvement.

On the other hand, it doesn't always make sense to gather feedback toward the end of the engagement. If a client has goals in areas where the work is less visible to others or will take a while to manifest outwardly, such as "practice greater self-compassion to support a calmer, more confident mindset," or "prioritize my work in a way that aligns with my values," it may not be helpful to collect feedback.

GATHERING PROGRESS FEEDBACK

If you and the client decide to collect progress feedback, discuss and agree to the process:

Who gathers the feedback? The client might want to have the conversations directly with stakeholders or may prefer that you collect the feedback.

Who provides the feedback? You and your client identify the right set of stakeholders to participate.

- Sometimes it's the same group who did the 360°; sometimes it's a subset, or a new set.
- Be sure to include colleagues in a position to observe the things the client is working on and those whose perceptions are essential.

When? Collect this feedback in time to debrief the client before asking them to do their final reflection and draft their Ongoing Development Plan so the feedback can inform their work.

How?

- This is a tighter data collection effort than the initial 360°; the focus is on how much and what progress the client has made on their coaching goals.
- With the client, review how you will articulate their goals to the stakeholders.
- You can use quick conversations, email, or a tool like SurveyMonkey.

Prepare the feedback to share in oral or written format. As you decide how best to format and share the results, consider your client's preferences (e.g., qualitative or quantitative, themes or examples).

SHARING AND PROCESSING PROGRESS FEEDBACK

Debriefing progress feedback is similar to the initial 360° debrief. (See Chapter 3: Assessments.) In addition:

- Help the client to be realistic about the amount of progress that's noticeable by others in this timeframe. Is it reasonable to expect that all participants would notice significant progress on all goals? Unlikely. So, if the client is shooting for 100 percent, help them see what's possible both in terms of their own change and others' ability to observe it.
- Support the client in identifying what pieces of constructive feedback feel most aligned with their observations and ongoing development; ask them to consider what will give them the most leverage. Then, support them in incorporat-

ing this feedback into their Ongoing Development Plan and letting the other feedback go for now. One client used the following sorting process for the constructive feedback received at completion:

a. No-Brainer: obvious and easy to implement. Start tomorrow.
b. Journey Ahead: aligns with my leadership journey and requires focus. Add it to my plan.
c. None of the Above: let it go.

FINAL REFLECTIONS AND ONGOING DEVELOPMENT PLAN

Taking the time to reflect on the coaching is an important step toward completion for the client. It's an opportunity to harvest learnings; notice what has changed and what has become habit; name successes; and codify the key behaviors, practices, and skills that have supported the client's progress (Cox 2010).

Some clients like to do this by writing out responses to a set of reflection questions; others prefer to respond to questions in conversation with the coach. Usually, we find a combination of the approaches works best to deepen the insights. It's important to capture the observations one way or another. Typically, this is the client's responsibility, as the cataloging reinforces ownership.

SAMPLE CLIENT FINAL REFLECTIONS

Marta's Final Coaching Reflections

1. What are you most proud of?
   Accepting hard feedback and using it to improve. Also, asking for help when I need it. Sticking with my intentions around spending time with my direct reports and delegating more to them.

2. What positive new beliefs do you have?
   The viewpoints of many lead to better decisions. Leaders who work through others instead of doing things themselves grow their team's capabilities and thus are able to elevate into more strategic activities.

3. How is your life different because of the things you have learned and worked on?
   I am more confident in my ability to set a vision and lead a team. I have greater trust in my team's abilities and am clear about their development trajectory. I now have time and a practice to step back, reflect, and think strategically.

4. How would you describe yourself as a leader now?
   Self-aware, informed, thoughtful, intentional (most of the time!)

5. What do you want to focus on as you continue to develop as a leader?
   Applying the skills and insights learned to larger-scale, cross-functional projects and to my peer relationships.

When it comes to self-assessing progress against the coaching plan, one of our colleagues, Amy Jen Su, shared the following model to explain and set expectations about the type and amount of progress that can happen over the course of a coaching engagement. This can be a useful frame to use with your client and sponsor:

1. **Awareness.** This is the earliest type of progress and may only be noticed by the client. It's an important first step given what we know about "awareness being self-correcting." (Learning stage: conscious incompetence)

2. **Adding to the Toolkit.** The client has actively experimented with and built some early competence in using new skills, habits, or tools. They have a growing understanding of when and how to use them. (Learning stage: conscious competence)

3. **Muscle Memory.** A new skill/habit/tool has been "stress-tested" and is now part of the client's repertoire; they know when/how to use it and they spend less effort—it starts to flow naturally. (Learning stage: unconscious competence)

In addition to looking back on the coaching to see progress and learnings, we work with the client to look ahead by building an Ongoing Development Plan. This plan integrates the learnings from coaching to sustain progress and a path forward for the client's ongoing development. This is a document the client will refer to in the future for reminders of what supports them being their best selves and keeping their growth and development on track. They may also use it to engage their sponsor in a conversation about their future development and how the sponsor can support it.

SAMPLE ONGOING DEVELOPMENT PLAN

B.K.'s Ongoing Development Plan

Leadership Vision: I commit to developing and leveraging a broader range of leadership tools so (1) my team members view me as an inclusive leader who supports and develops colleagues, and (2) the Executive Committee members see me as a confident and competent Head of Product.

Goal 1: Create a greater sense of team within the Product Management function.

- New Insights and Awareness:
  - Being transparent about the process is important; hearing from all team members fosters a sense of inclusion …
- Successes:
  - Colleague Feedback: "Now meetings include things like regular updates from SLT meetings, asking for everyone's input, recognizing people's contributions" …
- New Behaviors/Habits/Skills That Support My Success:
  - I have time on the calendar Tuesday and Thursday mornings to pause and reflect on what I need to share with my team from SLT and other cross-functional meetings I've attended; I ensure team meeting agendas have time for everyone to weigh in …
- Opportunities for Ongoing Development:
  - When busy or under deadline pressure, how to avoid backsliding to less communication …
- How I Will Maintain and Advance My Success on This Goal:
  - Ask my EA to double down on reflection time in my calendar in the weeks around a big deadline; ask two direct reports for feedback every quarter …

Clients may ask for your observations about their progress or suggestions about their path forward. Before responding, ask them for their observations, so they do their own reflection. This allows you to choose and position your comments to be of best service to the client.

—— THE FINAL SPONSOR MEETING ——

Here are some nuances of the final sponsor meeting to consider:

PREPARING THE CLIENT

Discuss how the client would like to show up in the meeting (i.e., what do they deliberately want to do or say in the meeting to demonstrate their growth? How can they prepare themselves for that?). There may be a direct tie back to the coaching plan (e.g., if the client is working on an aspect of executive presence or communication, then the meeting can be an opportunity to showcase the progress they've made). Talk about desired outcomes and how to structure the meeting to achieve those.

PREPARING THE SPONSOR

Like other sponsor meetings, it's useful to set expectations for the meeting: to share and celebrate successes and discuss how the client plans to maintain progress and continue developing. It's an opportunity to pass the baton from you, the formal coach, to the manager, now the informal coach.

TOP TIP: One of the most important things the coach can do is support the client and sponsor in agreeing on how they will work together to create accountability for executing the Ongoing Development Plan and ensure the client's development doesn't always take a back seat to business issues, a common challenge we observe.

CLOSING WITH THE CLIENT

You're nearly there! The last client coaching conversation includes most of these elements:

- Debrief the sponsor wrap-up
  - How did the client feel, what went well, what did they learn?
- Tweak the Ongoing Development Plan
  - What needs to be adjusted or clarified
  - Ensuring there is a concrete accountability strategy in place
  - Identifying anything else needed to support the client in the future
- Talk about the coach-client relationship post-conclusion
  - If a coaching tune-up meeting is part of the contract, agree on its timing, usually in two or three months. This meeting is to review how things are going against the Ongoing Development Plan, make any tweaks needed, and possibly explore any small coachable issues.
  - Talk about if or how you will stay in touch with the client, based on your practices and boundaries. You may wish to invite them to connect with you to share good news, ask you to be a quick sounding board, request a resource on a specific topic, and so on. You may also let the client know

that you'll be in touch from time to time and why, although each coach establishes their own boundaries around this.

TOP TIP: A clearly articulated accountability approach that engages others is one of the best gifts you can leave with the client. External accountability supports clients in paying attention to the changes they're making (Peterson 2007). Without a clear accountability strategy, clients can have a hard time executing their Ongoing Development Plan.

CLOSING WITH YOURSELF

In addition to closing with the client, we also take steps to honor the work we've done and harvest our own learnings:

1. Offer a gesture of completion. If it's your practice, share a gift that represents a significant learning or progress, or send a thoughtfully written note. For example:
   a. Eliza sends a handwritten note to her leaders a few weeks after wrapping up and shares what she learned from her client.
   b. Johan sends a small gift that is particular to each client. For example, Johan sent Lou a book of reflections because Lou had really appreciated and been moved by the reflection prompts Johan offered in coaching.
   c. Helen, taking inspiration from David Clutterbuck, plants a tree in honor of each client to symbolize their growth (Clutterbuck 2021).
2. Wrap up with HR. Take care of anything needed to formally close out the engagement.

3. For future marketing or "yay me!" reflection, you may invite the client to share a testimonial about working with you.

4. To codify learnings, summarize the engagement and capture your learnings (e.g., what was challenging, what you did well, what you would do differently next time).

5. Managing client notes is an essential part of intentional engagement. Different countries and companies have various regulations regarding this, as do the International Coaching Federation (ICF) and other coaching networks. Make time for clean-up work. At a minimum, our practices include shredding paper notes and deleting electronic files and emails two or three months post-completion.

6. Honor your work. Coaches may have practices or rituals for celebrating the good work they've done with a client. Examples we've heard or done ourselves include:

   a. The simple practice of moving the client's paper file or folder out of the Active Clients file, adding them to your "holiday card" address list, adding the client hours to any tally you keep for professional certification, or updating your coaching bio to include this work.

   b. Releasing the work through a long, hard run or hike.

   c. Making time to do something you love that gets you out of the office, such as golfing or spending time with friends.

   d. The generous act of making a charitable donation.

   e. The restorative practice of self-care—a special dinner, a massage, an outing.

It can be easy to neglect the work of **Ending With Meaning** given the bittersweet emotions, the attentional pull of new opportunities for you or your client, and your client's potentially flagging energy after the hard work of change, or in the rare case that an engagement has not gone as well as you hoped. But being intentional about these activities sets up your client for ongoing success.

○ ○ ○

CHAPTER 7 TAKEAWAYS

► A progress assessment and Ongoing Development Plan acknowledge the effort and ensure that benefits are captured as a useful reminder and guide to the client moving forward.

► The sponsor wrap-up meeting helps everyone acknowledge progress and recognize the value of the coaching investment. It also helps the organization know how to support the client's development in the future.

► Completion activities solidify your relationship with the client and the organization and maintain professionalism in the coaching.

FINISHING STRONG

○ ○ ○

We've now completed the arc of a coaching engagement, explored the Intentional Engagement Framework, and shared tools, structures, tips, and stories. Underpinning every part of the coaching engagement is the most important tool in your coaching toolkit: *you*.

The next chapters step away from the coaching engagement and address two topics for bringing your best *you* to your coaching work. Chapter 8 explores Coaching Presence and Chapter 9 explores Ongoing Development.

○ ○ ○

BEYOND THE ENGAGEMENT

CHAPTER 8

YOUR PRESENCE IS AN INTERVENTION: COACHING PRESENCE

R ecall a conversation when you felt connected and in tune with the other person, you were listening deeply, noticing body language and physical sensations, and letting go of any agenda you may have had. Really being with them and with the conversation, that's what we mean by presence. It is the act of attuning to ourselves and our client, of letting go of things outside of the coaching space to be with and witness to the client and our work with them.

This chapter explores how to develop your capacity for presence, the impact of your presence on others, and the practices and structures that support your ability to be present with clients as well as help your clients be present.

COACHING PRESENCE: KEY ELEMENTS

- Cultivating your presence
- Presence as an intervention
- Being present with clients
- Helping clients build presence

CULTIVATING YOUR PRESENCE

If you want to be physically strong, you work at it regularly, logging hours with the right workouts, a range of equipment and, possibly, a trainer. Likewise, if you want to strengthen your presence, you need to practice regularly and build habits to support it. Doug Silsbee writes that presence is available to anyone, at any time; it can be intentionally and systematically cultivated to overcome patterns and tendencies that cut off access to it. It follows that the more you develop your presence, the more available it will be in challenging situations.

Building presence is a continuous journey and workout. As we grow in our capacity and skills as a coach, our presence needs to grow and deepen as well. As our colleague and teacher Joy Leach wisely pointed out, "In order to be present to the client, I need to be present to my own shadow right now, to my bias, to my need. That's a lot of being present! That's a lot of channels open."

Being present to ourselves requires us to get to know ourselves deeply and integrate different parts of ourselves. Thus we become more aware of our shadows, unseen motivations, and unnamed triggers. Bringing this into focus helps us reduce internal distractions and unconscious filters as we work with clients. When we talked with coaches about how they develop and maintain presence, each shared a highly personal approach. The practices they named included:

1. **Reflective practices.** Journaling, meditation, contemplative reading, poetry, intention setting, mindfulness study, labyrinth walking
2. **Body practices.** Yoga, aikido, tai chi, breathing, embodiment or somatic exercises
3. **Restorative practices.** Reiki, acupuncture, massage, retreats

Any of these practices can work for any one of us. What's important is exploring what works for you and is sustainable on a regular basis, and ensuring you regularly check in with yourself to refresh practices when needed.

PRESENCE AS AN INTERVENTION

Dorothy Siminovitch coined the phrase "your presence is an intervention." In short, being present, showing up with intentionality, and paying attention to another person influences that person. Research confirms that human beings affect one another's energetic systems (McCraty, Atkinson, and Tiller 1999). A calm, centered presence, unfettered by the myriad things we might be carrying (e.g., a difficult morning in the dentist's chair or an exciting work inquiry), invites our client to join us in a space that supports meaningful, connected coaching. Conversely, when our system is activated, it can hijack our client's system, and vice versa. Being aware of this dynamic enables us to notice when it's happening, come back to center, and be intentional about maintaining our presence.

Invitation to Settle

Robin's client, Jen, arrived late for their first meeting apologetic, flustered, and anxious. Robin remained centered and calm while Jen settled into her chair. Once Jen was seated, Robin suggested they take a few full, slow breaths together before beginning the session. Jen agreed, and Robin invited her to close her eyes and led her through a breathing exercise. As the exercise concluded, Jen opened her eyes and her energy was distinctly different as she engaged in the conversation.

Several months later during their mid-engagement check-in meeting, Robin was pleased to hear Jen share how much that first session affected her. "I was such a mess, and you were so calm," Jen said. "Your energy and pace calmed me and gave me the grace and space to settle down. That made such a difference."

It is rare, in the busyness of today's world, for a person to experience what it's like to be the focus of another person's deep attention. Bringing ourselves to presence, and helping our clients to presence themselves, is an important aspect of creating the space and wisdom for the deeper work of coaching to happen. Presence allows you to be attuned to the client and listen at multiple levels to what is and isn't being communicated. When a coach is fully present, it is more likely that the client feels a connection. They feel heard. It's a different quality of conversation than they typically have on a day-to-day basis. Your presence as a coach can encourage the client to be present to themselves, their experience, and their unspoken feelings and intuition.

What happens when we get present to ourselves and our clients in coaching?

- Coaches and clients have greater awareness, tapping into more resources, emotions, intuitions, and insights about themselves and their situations (Passmore and Marianetti 2007).
- There's a stronger connection and more psychological safety between coach and client, allowing for deeper exploration.
- Our work is less effortful; we become a channel for the work, and the questions flow through us.

BEING PRESENT WITH CLIENTS

We grow our capacity for presence using various practices outside of coaching sessions. How then do we bring this presence into coaching? What do we and others do before, during, and after coaching conversations to stay present, clear, and attuned to the client and the coaching agenda?

BEFORE COACHING CONVERSATIONS

Many coaches have a personal practice for centering before a client meeting. Here are three useful approaches to consider weaving into your coaching preparation:

- Set an intention for this conversation. How do you want to be with the client during this conversation? The intention could be a word, a phrase, or an image that helps tap into the presence you want to embody. Here are some examples:
  1. With a client who's having a hard time processing a recent performance review, an intention might be "safe, compassionate, balanced."
  2. With a client who's practicing a difficult conversation they're anxious about, an intention could be "yellow belt practice partner," signifying a presence that's firm and challenging but not overpowering the way a black belt practice partner would be.
  3. A more general intention you might call on is an image of standing shoulder to shoulder with a client looking out at a complex landscape to be navigated.

- Be mindful of your triggers and apply Dan Siegel's "name it to tame it" concept, by taking a few moments to reflect and name potential triggers. Externalizing emotionally potent experiences brings a sense of clarity and greater control (Siegel and Bryson 2012). It heightens our ability to be present to ourselves and our clients. Before a session consider:
  1. What has triggered you before with this client? (e.g., impatience when you hear a lack of action taken between coaching conversations)
  2. What's your current state of emotion and energy? How easily might you be triggered today?
  3. What do you want to let go of as you enter into the coaching space?

- Center yourself. This includes things such as breathing techniques, embodiment practices, or meditation. One of our favorites comes from Wendy and Tiphani Palmer of Leadership Embodiment (Palmer and Crawford 2013). The steps are simply to:
  1. Inhale, lengthening up your spine
  2. Exhale, softening down your front and thinking of someone, something, someplace that makes you smile
  3. Expand your personal space to fill the room
  4. Settle into the space around you

Additionally before a coaching conversation, clear your workspace of distractions—phone ringer and message alerts off, turning away from your screens if you're meeting by phone; and if meeting in person, choosing a seat in the room that allows the least distraction for your client. The practice of arriving a few minutes early provides the time to do a final centering practice, like a few mindful breaths, before stepping into coaching.

We've also learned that when we're tired, or hungry, or in some other way have not attended to our own needs, it's harder to maintain presence, so we take that into account as we prepare, and even as we schedule our days. One coach we know always carries a bag of nuts with her when she's on the client site so she can quickly fuel up between meetings, as avoiding hunger supports her capacity for presence.

DURING COACHING CONVERSATIONS

Some coaches interpret being fully present as a singular focus on their client. This approach misses an important element— attending to yourself.

If your focus is completely external, you miss the opportunity to notice shifts in your own presence over the course of the conversation. Patrick Casement describes the distinction between our "observing self" and "experiencing self" as the ability to look objectively at our thoughts and feelings while also experiencing them (Bluckert 2006). As a coach, this translates into being fully engaged with your client while also maintaining awareness of yourself. This enables you to notice and adjust if you are feeling triggered. It also enables you to notice feelings and reactions to the client that may be useful to reflect back to them.

Buzzes and Keystrokes and Beeps, Oh My!

It was Maddie's second coaching conversation with Jan, a newly promoted CTO. Maddie had thoughtfully prepared for the meeting, reviewing her notes and reflection from last time, and taking several minutes to center. She felt calm, clear, and energized for the work with Jan. Fifteen minutes into the conversation, she noticed she was feeling distracted and irritated. She paused to check in with herself and realized that the beeps, buzzes, and keystroke sounds coming from Jan's side of the Zoom were making it difficult to concentrate on the conversation. Jan's eyes wandered all over the screen and it was obvious that her attention wasn't fully on the coaching. Maddie knew they couldn't do their best work in these conditions, so she shared her observation. This led to a rich conversation about the weight of expectations Jan was feeling, the pressure to constantly multitask, and the impact of this on Jan and others. Together they explored options for Jan to experiment with and agreed on how they wanted to interact in the future.

At first it can be awkward to tune in to your client while also attending to your own experience of the conversation. With deliberate practice, it becomes a more fluid process of being aware of yourself while also staying connected with your client and what they're sharing. If you find that you're having a hard time staying present with your client, use this as information and get curious about it. Notice when you're drifting off or when strong emotions arise, or when you simply don't feel connected to the client. Ask yourself if that lack of presence is something to raise with the client in the moment or something to manage for yourself, or important data for you about what's happening in the coaching relationship. Make a quick note to yourself about this, then shift your attention back to your client.

On the other hand, if you find yourself only focusing on your client and not checking in with yourself from time to time, that's something to attend to. Your coaching intuition comes from being aware of yourself and your experience as well as your clients. Some things we've learned to notice and attend to for ourselves:

- Clenching or tightness of muscles
- Shallow breaths
- Fidgeting in the seat, or with your hands or feet
- A nagging sense of a question—perhaps your intuition is trying to make itself known
- The push or pull of an emotion—possibly felt as a "red flag" of worry or fear

It's helpful to remind ourselves that during client conversations, we're constantly managing both intention and attention.

AFTER COACHING CONVERSATIONS

Coaching conversations can be intense. Following a coaching conversation, it can be useful to check in with yourself. Is there residual energy that you need to release rather than carry it forward?

- Brianna schedules five minutes after every coaching call to breathe, drink water, and come back to being present to herself. She lets go of anything from the previous conversation by vigorously shaking her hands and arms to release it.
- Joe makes time over lunch and at the end of the day for a quick walk or stretch to reconnect with his body. Afterwards he reflects on the conversations of the day.
- Suzanne takes time to notice her energy and name it, then she intentionally lets it go.

As we describe in Chapter 5, it's helpful to capture post-session reflections, and we often include insights on presence. This allows you to identify patterns in your work over time, and any work you want to do around building your presence muscles and practices. Following are questions to support this reflection:

- What was easy or hard about being present to yourself and your client?
- How did your intention serve you?
- What is the relationship between your centering practice and the quality of the coaching?

HELPING CLIENTS BUILD PRESENCE

Have you worked with a client who was so stuck on a recent interaction or event, almost like having a conversational hangover, that they had a hard time being present in your coaching session? Sometimes clients need our help to get present before they can fully engage in a coaching conversation. You know how this looks and feels; for example, a client's energy nearly jumps across the desk at you as they sit down and start talking a hundred miles an hour. What then?

Some clients will appreciate you suggesting that you take a few breaths together to land in the room, ready for coaching. Others are accepting, even eager, for more. One client we worked with requested that we lead a guided five-minute meditation at the start of each coaching conversation, as it was the only time in her week for meditation.

On the other hand, some clients might say or give off the vibe that they are wary of anything they perceive as "woo woo." In this case, you might share with them that studies have shown that presence or mindfulness practices positively affect well-being, engagement, and performance (Eby et al. 2019). Alternatively, using language such as "Would you be willing to try something different today as we start and see how it works for us?" makes for a lighter, possibly more appealing introduction to the idea. Rarely has a client been opposed to trying something new at least once.

Here are a couple of quick approaches to help a client increase their presence at the start of, or even in the middle of, a coaching conversation:

- Taking several full breaths in and out through the nose, paying attention to the temperature and sensation of the air flow in their nostrils, noticing any differences on the inhalation and exhalation.
- Quickly scanning the body from head to toe to notice where there might be some tightness or tension, then taking a few deep breaths into that place to relax the tension.
- Asking the client to "clear their cache" by taking two or three minutes to write down everything on their mind.

Swipe Up!

Jess was working with John, a successful leader in the banking industry who struggled with presence in and out of coaching sessions. John described his challenge as an inability to turn his brain off. He was constantly ruminating on problems or issues that needed to be solved. One day Jess hit on a useful analogy. She suggested that John think about his constant rumination like an app that's open on his iPhone. Even if he wasn't using the app, it was constantly draining energy from his phone. John immediately got it, and they landed on the metaphor of "swiping up" as a way for John to disrupt his rumination. In their next session John was so energized by his progress he started sharing before he even sat down. "Swiping up totally works! I tried to catch myself every time I started getting distracted and then thought 'swipe up' and was able to let go and focus my attention on the topic or person in front of me!" It is a practice he uses to this day ... and Jess does too.

Coaching is often the only time a busy client has to pause and reflect, so helping them increase their presence can lead to deeper, more meaningful work. It also supports them in learning how to be present outside of coaching. Clients often mention that they take the centering work we do in coaching into other meetings and situations, like pausing between back-to-back meetings to take full breaths and tune in to themselves before stepping into the next meeting room or reminding themselves to "be where their feet are" during a meeting they find hard to pay attention to.

In a world of near-constant distraction, cultivating and demonstrating presence can be a superpower for leaders. As you do this sort of work with clients, it supports their ability to be more present and intentional about their presence.

A FEW FAVORITE RESOURCES

There's a wealth of books, classes, and retreats aimed at cultivating presence, aka mindfulness, with sources from ancient wisdom to new findings from neuroscience. Below are a few of our favorite resources and teachers:

- *A Gestalt Coaching Primer: The Path towards Awareness Intelligence,* Dorothy Siminovitch
- *Leadership Embodiment,* Wendy Palmer
- *Presence: Human Purpose and the Field of the Future* by Peter Senge, Otto Scharmer, and Joseph Jaworski
- *Presence-Based Coaching,* Doug Silsbee
- *Self as Coach, Self as Leader,* Pamela McLean (Chapter 4 in particular)
- *The Book of Awakening,* Mark Nepo
- *Your Body Is Your Brain,* Amanda Blake
- The Strozzi Institute

CHAPTER 8 TAKEAWAYS

▶ Presence is a capability and capacity that must be developed. Just like a professional athlete works out at the gym, not just during games. It takes regular practice outside of the "coaching arena" to build, strengthen, and maintain presence.

▶ Your presence itself is a coaching intervention. How you show up and how you engage your client impacts the work itself.

▶ It's important to have practices before, during, and after coaching conversations that help you to focus on your presence.

▶ Supporting clients to get present during coaching conversations helps them build important muscles and skills they can use outside of coaching.

CHAPTER 9

YOU ARE YOUR OWN BEST TOOL: ONGOING DEVELOPMENT FOR COACHES

As coaches, we have chosen a profession dedicated to supporting the development of others, so it is not surprising that we tend to be deeply committed to our own ongoing development. When you bring a group of coaches together, the conversation will inevitably shift to the books we are reading, the podcasts we're listening to, and the classes and supervision we're attending.

Learning and development opportunities for coaches seem to be everywhere, which is exciting and sometimes overwhelming. How do you determine which activities will have the greatest impact? What types of development make the most sense for you based on your experience and the clients you work with? How do you manage your investment of time and resources to yield the most benefit? These are all critical aspects of a coach's ongoing development following the completion of their initial certification program.

ONGOING DEVELOPMENT FOR COACHES: KEY ELEMENTS

- Categories of development
- Coaching supervision
- Creating an ongoing development strategy
- Learning in community

CATEGORIES OF DEVELOPMENT

To help navigate the many opportunities out there and simplify this discussion, we have organized the coach development universe into three categories that cover both horizontal development (expanding your toolkit) and vertical development (expanding your mindset):

1. Self-development

Each coach brings unique talents and perspectives to their client work. They also bring their own stories, shadows, fears, motivations, and assumptions (to name a few). If we do not do our own work to increase our self-awareness and understanding (e.g., identifying and working with shadows), we will coach through a cloudy lens. Doing the work to understand ourselves helps us have perspective on our conditioning and operate from a place of awareness and choice. Thus we are less likely to be triggered by, react to, or collude with our clients.

As we have pursued our own self-development, we have benefited from countless frameworks and models, including Robert Kegan's stages of adult development, Wendy Palmer's Leadership Embodiment work, and the Enneagram.

THE SELF AS COACH MODEL

In addition to these development frameworks and models, we frequently refer to a self-development model unique to coaches put forth in the book *Self as Coach, Self as Leader* by Pamela McLean. The Self as Coach model focuses on six dimensions that are essential to coaches (see illustration).

McLean's work is both rich and accessible, providing the what and the why for each dimension. It also provides ways for the reader to self-assess and identify strengths and areas to focus on. We return to this model time and time again to inform our ongoing reflection and development.

We describe other types of self-development in the table that follows. This category is difficult to put clear boundaries around; self-as-coach is always enriched by the other types of development. After all, how can you gain certification in an assessment tool (which inevitably requires you to self-assess) or engage in coaching training without turning the lens on yourself?

2. **Expanding and strengthening your coaching capabilities**
Once a coach has completed their initial certification program, they continue to build their capabilities and competency as a coach. This may occur in informal ways such as reading books, listening to podcasts, and participating in peer-to-peer coaching. Formal development programs, defined as expert-led learning experiences, focus on elevating the coach's overall capabilities or targeting a specific coaching approach.

CATEGORIES AND EXAMPLES OF COACH DEVELOPMENT*

SELF-DEVELOPMENT	EXPANDING & STRENGTHENING COACHING CAPABILITIES	COACHING TOOLS & FRAMEWORKS		
		LEADERSHIP ASSESSMENTS	DIAGNOSTIC TOOLS	FRAMEWORKS & TOOLS TO SUPPORT A COACHING CONVERSATION
• Creativity classes • Embodiment/ Somatics • Reflection workshops with thought leaders (e.g., Mark Nepo) • Self as coach work ...	• Brain-based coaching programs • Depth coaching programs • Master coach programs • Positive psychology degree programs ...	• Be Well, Lead Well • Hogan Assessments • The Leadership Circle Profile • The Leadership Effectiveness Analysis ...	• Clifton Strengths • DiSC • Enneagram • EQ in Action • Insights Discovery • Myers-Briggs Type Indicator ...	• Daring Greatly • Immunity to Change • Metaphor Magic • Neuro-Linguistic Programming • Theory U ...

DEVELOPMENT ACTIVITIES THAT OFFER ENRICHMENT ACROSS CATEGORIES:
Coaching Conferences (e.g., ICF Converge, EMCC Global Coaching & Supervision Conference, etc.)
Coaching Supervision (1:1 or group)

Not intended as an exhaustive list

3. Coaching tools and frameworks

This third category of development opportunities includes the infinite tools and frameworks available to support a coaching engagement. We have organized them into three subcategories:

- Leadership assessment tools
- Diagnostic tools
- Frameworks and tools to support the coaching conversation

By offering these categories, we hope to help you navigate the possibilities for yourself, being deliberate about where you're spending your time and energy, and not getting stuck in a single lane of development. We'll talk more about crafting a learning journey later in this chapter.

COACHING SUPERVISION

We can't imagine doing our best coaching without being in coaching supervision. After many years in supervision, and one of us trained and certified as a supervisor, we deeply believe in having a safe environment in which to reflect on our experience and learn.

Coaching supervision emerged in the UK in the early 2000s. Its premise is that, like other client-based practices such as social work, psychology, and psychiatry that work under strict confidentiality, coaches require a mechanism to continue their development, talking about their cases in a safe, supportive, and confidential environment.

However, the term "coaching supervision" can be misleading, as the role of a coaching supervisor is not to provide approval or judgment. Instead, think of a supervisor as a partner who will join and support you in conversations focused on developing and deepening your coaching. The objective is to help you gain "SUPER-vision" about your work.

Working with a coaching supervisor is different than having a conversation with a coaching colleague. Supervisors have completed an extensive training and certification process that enables them to create a supportive space for coaches to reflect on their client work and explore it, and themselves, through multiple lenses.

Peter Hawkins and Nick Smith describe the three focal areas of coaching supervision as:

- Development: Expanding your capacity as a coach by building skills (e.g., exploring different ways of working) and deepening understanding of self (e.g., why you react to a client in a certain way)
- Resourcing: Building awareness of how client work can affect coaches and increasing their capacity for self-care
- Qualitative: Reflecting and supporting the professional and ethical standards of coaching (Hawkins and Smith 2006)

These focal areas translate into supervision as a coach takes the time to pause and reflect on their practice either 1:1 with a supervisor or in group supervision sessions led by a coaching supervisor. You may discuss something that has gone well in an engagement so you can focus on bringing more of what works into your coaching. You might look at situations that did not go well with the goal of discovery and growth. Finally, it is a space to work on developing yourself, exploring how you can increase self-awareness and bring your best self to coaching engagements.

Growing research points to coaches at every stage of development—from emerging coaches to very experienced ones—benefiting from the learning that comes from coaching supervision (Downing 2021). Supervision is a formal requirement for coaching certification for members of EMCC but is less well known in the US. This is changing, as the ICF now recognizes coaching supervision as an important form of development, and coaches are able to submit some coaching supervision hours as CCEUs toward their ICF certification requirement.

CREATING A DEVELOPMENT STRATEGY

Every coach we know is involved in some form of continuous development. This is because development for a coach is not a "nice to have," it is a "must have." *We* are the most critical tool in our toolbox and should continuously invest in our development to keep that tool in the best possible condition for coaching. Learning is often driven by the coach's current curiosity or interests and frequently yields an idea, tool, or framework that can be applied to current engagements.

We find that thinking about our development intentionally and creating a development strategy, even an informal one, increases our commitment and follow-through. Some coaches we know pick a focus for the year, such as immersion into a tool like the Enneagram, a skill like Embodiment, or a current leadership topic like Diversity & Inclusion. Others seek the variety and stimulation of a more diverse set of experiences. David Clutterbuck suggests having a 12-to-18-month plan that's informed by reflecting on your coaching path (Clutterbuck 2019).

Following are questions to consider as you create your development plan:

1. What development will make me a better coach for my clients?
2. What feedback am I getting from clients about my coaching and how can that inform my development plan?
3. Are there tools or frameworks a client organization (or my organization) would like me to use?
4. What are the opportunities to learn with my colleagues and build community?
5. What topics are most interesting to me right now?
6. Where do I want to take my coaching practice in the next few years and what learning will support me in achieving that?
7. What will give me the most "bang for my buck"?

Each coach's learning journey is unique, based on who they are, their experience prior to becoming a coach, and the type of work that they're doing. Development is also influenced by the coach's tenure:

- A new coach is likely to focus on creating a foundation—selecting development opportunities that enable them to have the baseline assessments, frameworks, and approaches that will support their coaching.
- An experienced coach who has already built this foundation may seek development in more specialized areas.

We notice that our own learning journeys have a natural ebb and flow driven by our interests and our capacity. Some periods are for exploring new areas of interest, others are defined by intense learning, and still others are for integration of learning.

LEARNING IN COMMUNITY

From the outside, an observer might view coaching as a connected profession; after all, coaches spend their days engaging with clients and building relationships. However, coaching is in many ways a solitary endeavor, because the client relationships we build are professional and primarily focused on our client. While clients and coaches feel connected and engaged with one another, coaches do not share their professional or personal lives with their clients. In other words, we are there for them; they are not (and should not be) there for us. For this reason, most coaches actively build connection and community with other coaches. One way we do this is by learning in community.

There have been so many times when we have texted coaching colleagues to ask for a few minutes to confidentially process something happening in our coaching practice. We value being able to connect with a trusted colleague to explore a challenging situation, discuss how to use a tool or hear another's perspective on it, or just enjoy a sense of camaraderie that someone else has faced a similar situation. We deliberately build our network as a means of learning and growth as well as a source of connection and collegiality.

Coaches begin building community in their initial coach certification experience. Coaching certification is an intense and often vulnerable experience requiring individuals who have been successful in their careers to go back to a beginner's stance. Now layer in that many coaching programs ask students to build awareness of their own areas of development, which requires a high degree of introspection. This experience bonds the participants and often forms the nucleus of a coach's community. We know of many small learning groups who have continued meeting for years after their coaching certification program concluded. Other groups form around a shared experience or need after they have completed their initial training.

Learning events, certification programs, and coaching conferences also serve as a way to connect with our coaching colleagues and meet new colleagues. These connections often lead to continuing discussions after the event, deepening the learning. Many global forums provide these opportunities, such as the International Coaching Federation (ICF), European Mentoring and Coaching Council (EMCC), Institute of Coaching (IOC), World Business & Executive Coach Summit (WBECS), and Coaches Rising. For more local connections, try exploring offerings from the regional and country-based chapters of ICF and EMCC.

Peer coaching, when two or more people who share common goals collaborate to help each other become successful in their work, is another effective way of learning in community (McDermott 2012). Peer coaching may happen in a structured, regular manner with clearly articulated ways of engaging, or ad hoc, like picking up the phone to call a coaching colleague when you're feeling stuck.

Coaching supervision groups are also a strong source of learning and community. Because of the nature of supervision conversations, group members form close relationships and a high degree of trust. Groups typically start by contracting for six or twelve months of supervision and then recontract to continue. Many of them stay intact for years, valuing the close bonds and high trust built over time and shared experience. For example, Laura has spent the last six years in the same group of coaches who meet virtually twice a month. She credits her supervision group as the single most important lever for increasing her coaching capacity and deepening her learning of Self as Coach.

As we wrote this book we were reminded many times of the power of learning in community—from our 1:1 conversations with each other, our small group conversations, and our supervision groups. We encourage you to experiment with and find what works for you, then stick with it, invest in it, and grow!

CHAPTER 9 TAKEAWAYS

▶ Your initial coaching certification program is the launch of your development journey as a coach and a starting point for building your learning community.

▶ To be at their best, coaches continually focus on their development, leveraging informal and formal learning opportunities.

▶ Creating a development strategy enables a coach to think intentionally about their capabilities and how they would like to evolve. It also serves as a checkpoint to evaluate investment and impact.

▶ Each coach's learning journey will be unique. How you choose to approach your ongoing development is up to you; we encourage you to just make sure to do it.

▶ Learning is a wonderful way for coaches to be connected in community. Coaches often share ideas and new development opportunities, as well as deepen their learning through informal and formal discussion groups.

AFTERWORD

As we finished writing this book, we found ourselves reflecting on our initial motivations for jumping into this mostly joyful and sometimes challenging creative journey:

- Easing the way for others by sharing our hard-earned lessons and wisdom
- Helping new coaches minimize uncertainty and increase confidence as they launch their coaching practices
- Encouraging experienced coaches to reflect on their practice, consider new approaches, and experiment with what captures their imagination, and,
- Contributing to raising the quality of coaching in the world

We have learned so much along the way, from interviews with talented coach colleagues, diving into the research, and our daily discussions as we collaborated on *Do Your Best Coaching*. Our coaching is even better today than it was a year ago, having paused to consider how we're working, where we've fallen into habit instead of deliberate practice, and where we can infuse new approaches we've learned along the way.

Our hope is that this book and the Intentional Engagement Framework will serve as a launching point for your own exploration and conversations across your coaching community. That they will prompt you to be curious about your own practice, regardless of your years of experience. And that in doing so, you will find new ways of working that support your best, most skillful and fully resourced coaching. We'd love to hear from you and keep this dialogue going.

Julie & Laura
www.doyourbestcoaching.com

REFERENCES

Alvey, Susan, and Kathleen Barclay. 2007. "The Characteristics of Dyadic Trust in Executive Coaching." *Journal of Leadership Studies* 1 (1): 18–27. https://doi.org/10.1002/jls.20004.

Anderson, Robert J., and William A. Adams. 2016. *Mastering Leadership: An Integrated Framework for Breakthrough Performance and Extraordinary Business Results.* Hoboken: Wiley.

Anseel, Frederik, Adam S. Beatty, Winny Shen, Filip Lievens, and Paul R. Sackett. 2015. "How Are We Doing After 30 Years? A Meta-Analytic Review of the Antecedents and Outcomes of Feedback-Seeking Behavior." *Journal of Management* 41 (1): 318–348.

Blake, Amanda. 2018. *Your Body Is Your Brain.* Trokay Press.

Bluckert, Peter. 2006. *Psychological Dimensions of Executive Coaching.* Berkshire: Open University Press.

Burger, Zelda, and Salome van Coller-Peter. 2019. "A Guiding Framework for Multi-Stakeholder Contracting in Executive Coaching." *SA Journal of Human Resource Management* 17 (1): 1–11. https://doi.org/10.4102/sajhrm.v17i0.1114.

Casement, Peter. 1985. *On Learning from the Patient.* Hove: Brunner-Routledge.

Clutterbuck, David. 2019. "Creating Your Coach Development Plan." *David Clutterbuck Partnership.* https://davidclutterbuckpartnership.com/creating-your-coach-development-plan/.

Clutterbuck, David and Michael Hudson. 2021. "A Wise Conversation: David Clutterbuck & Michael Hudson: Radical Renewal Conference. Virtual Session.

Collins, Padraig, and Jessica R. Nesmer-Magnus. 2010. "Measuring Shared Team Mental Models: A Meta-Analysis." *Group Dynamics: Theory, Research, and Practice* 14 (1): 1–14. https://doi.org/10.1037/a0017455.

Cox, Elaine. 2010. "Last Things First: Ending Well in the Coaching Relationship." In *The Coaching Relationship: Putting People First,* by Chris and Almuth McDowall Smewing, 159–178. New York: Routledge.

De Hann, Erik, and Anna Duckworth. 2021. "The Coaching Relationship and Other Common Factors in Executive Coaching Outcome." In *Coaching Relationships: The Relational Coaching Field Book*, by Erik and Charlotte Sills DeHann. Oxfordshire: Libri Publishing.

De Hann, Erik, Yvonne D. Burger, Anthony M. Grant, and Per-Olof Eriksson. 2016. "A large-scale study of executive and workplace coaching: The relative contributions of relationship, personality match, and self-efficacy." *Consulting Psychology Journal: Practice and Research* 68 (3): 189–207.

DeChurch, Leslie A., and Jessica R. Mesmer-Magnus. 2010. "Measuring Shared Team Mental Models: A Meta-Analysis." *Group Dynamics: Theory, Research, and Practice* 14 (1): 1–14.

Downing, Kathryn. 2021. *Creating the Container for Reflective Practice in Virtual Small Group Supervision.* PhD Dissertation, Middlesex University.

Eby, Lilian T., Tammy D. Allen, Kate M. Conley, Rachel L. Williamson, Tyler G. Henderson, and Victor S. Mancini. 2019. "Mindfulness-based training interventions for employees: A qualitative review of the literature." *Human Resource Management Review* 29 (2): 156–178.

Glenn, Rebecca, Penny Handscomb, Amy Kosterlitz, Kathleen Marron, Kelly Ross, Lori Siegworth, and Timothy Signorelli. 2019. *Fearless Feedback: A Guide for Coaching Leaders to See Themselves More Clearly and Galvanize Growth.* Minneapolis: Master Coach Authors' Press.

Goldsmith, Marshall, and Howard Morgan. 2004. "Leadership Is a Contact Sport." *strategy + business*, August 25, 2004. https://www.strategy-business.com/article/04307.

Hannafey, Francis T., and Lawrence A. Vitulano. 2013. "Ethics and Executive Coaching: An Agency Theory Approach." *Journal of Business Ethics* 115 (2013): 599–603. https://doi.org/10.1007/s10551-012-1442-z.

Hawkins, Peter, and Nick Smith. 2006. *Coaching, Mentoring and Organizational Consulting, Supervision and Development.* Maidenhead: Open University Press.

Kauffman, Carol, and Diane Coutu. 2009. "The Realities of Executive Coaching." *Harvard Business Review: HBR Research Report*, January

2009. https://edbatista.typepad.com/files/realities_of_executive_coaching_hbr.pdf.

Kegan, Robert. 1994. *In Over Our Heads: The Mental Demands of Modern Life.* Cambridge: Harvard University Press.

Kombarakaran, Francis A., et al. 2008. "Executive Coaching: It Works." *Consulting Psychology Journal: Practice and Research* 60 (1): 78–90. https://doi.org/10.1037/1065-9293.60.1.78.

McCarthy, Alma M. 1999. "Developing Self-Awareness in the Managerial Career Development Process: The Value of 360-degree Feedback and the MBTI." *Journal of European Industrial Training* 23 (9): 437–445. https://doi.org/10.1108/03090599910302613.

McCraty, Rollin, Mike Atkinson, and William Tiller. 1999. "The role of physiological coherence in the detection and measurement of cardiac energy exchange between people." *Proceedings of the Tenth International Montreux Congress on Stress.* Montreux.

McDermott, Lynda. 2012. "Tapping the Wisdom of Peers." *T + D* 66 (5): 70–72.

McLean, Pamela. 2019. *Self as Coach, Self as Leader: Developing the Best in You to Develop the Best in Others.* Hoboken: John Wiley & Sons.

Palmer, Wendy, and Janet Crawford. 2013. *Leadership Embodiment.* CreateSpace.

Passarelli, Angela M. 2015. "Vision-Based Coaching: Optimizing Resources for Leader Development." *Frontiers in Psychology* 15 (April 2015). https://doi.org/10.3389/fpsyg.2015.00412.

Passmore, Jonathan, and Oberdan Marianetti. 2007. "The Role of Mindfulness in Coaching." *The Coaching Psychologist* 3 (3): 131–137.

Payne, Stephanie C., Satoris S. Youngcourt, and J. Matthew Beaubien. 2007. "A Meta-Analytic Examination of the Goal Orientation Nomological Net." *Journal of Applied Psychology* 92 (1): 128–150. https://doi.org/10.1037/0021-9010.92.1.128.

Peterson, David. 2007. "Executive Coaching in a Cross-Cultural Context." *Consulting Psychology Journal: Practice & Research* 59 (4): 261–271. https://doi.org/10.1037/1065-9293.59.4.261.

Pliopas, Ana. 2021. "Executive Coaching: Managing Relationships Between Coach, Client and Organization." Converge '21 online session, October 27, 2021.

Saporito, Thomas J. 1996. "Business-Linked Executive Development: Coaching Senior Executives." *Consulting Psychology Journal: Practice and Research* 48 (2): 96–103. https://doi.org/10.1037/1061-4087.48.2.96.

Seijits, Gerard H., and Gary P. Latham. 2005. "Learning versus Performance Goals: When Should Each Be Used." *Academy of Management Perspectives* 19 (1): 124–131. https://doi.org/10.5465/ame.2005.15841964.

Senge, Peter M., C. Otto Scharmer, Joseph Jaworski, and Betty Sue Flowers. 2004. *Presence: An Exploration of Profound Change.* Society for Organizational Learning, Doubleday.

Sieck, Whitney. 2020. "A Sales Enablement Blueprint for Success." *Talent Development* 74 (5): 42–47. https://www.td.org/magazines/td-magazine/a-sales-enablement-blueprint-for-success.

Siegel, Daniel J., and Tina P. Bryson. 2012. *The Whole-Brain Child.* New York: Delacorte Press.

Silsbee, Doug. 2008. *Presence-Based Coaching.* San Francisco: Jossey-Bass.

Smewing, Chris, and Almuth McDowall. 2010. "Assessment in Coaching." In *The Coaching Relationship: Putting People First,* by Stephen and Almuth McDowall Palmer, 97–118. New York: Routledge.

Spence, Gordon B. 2007. "GAS Powered coaching: Goal Attainment Scaling and Its Use in Coaching Research and Practice." *International Coaching Psychology Review* 2 (2): 155–167.

Starr, Julie. 2021. *The Coaching Manual (5th ed.).* London: Pearson Business.

Thach, Elizabeth C. 2002. "The Impact of Executive Coaching and 360 Feedback on Leadership Effectiveness." *Leadership & Organization Development Journal* 23 (4): 205–214. https://doi.org/10.1108/01437730210429070.

Welsh, David T., Michael D. Baer, and Hudson Sessions. 2020. "Hot Pursuit: The Affective Consequences of Organizational-Set Versus Self-Set Goals for Emotional Exhaustion and Citizenship Behavior." *Journal of Applied Psychology* 105 (2): 166–185. https://doi.org/10.1037/apl0000429.

APPENDIX

STICKY SITUATIONS MATRIX

The Sticky Situations below are those that may be prevented or mitigated by applying the Intentional Engagement Framework's processes and tools.

Many of these situations will also require your coaching skills to navigate, and here are some thoughts on how process and tools can also support you in navigating or even preventing these.

		STICKY SITUATION	WHERE WE COVER IT
CREATING THE CONTAINER		**You're Being Pulled Into a Rescue Mission**	
	1	Your client's organization uses coaching in a way that is not aligned with the work you do; e.g., "rescue mission" or "last resort" coaching.	Chapter 1: Putting Your Best Foot Forward Chapter 2: Starting Strong
		You did not start strong and regret it	
	2	You feel pressure to start coaching without a signed contract.	Chapter 1: Putting Your Best Foot Forward Chapter 2: Starting Strong
	3	You forego or skip aspects of intake and kickoff because your client needed to jump right into coaching but now feel you missed critical information and relationship building.	Chapter 2: Starting Strong
	4	You're at or over capacity and a potential client wants to start right away.	Chapter 1: Putting Your Best Foot Forward Chapter 2: Starting Strong Chapter 5: Being Intentional

STICKY SITUATION	WHERE WE COVER IT
YOU'RE BEING CHALLENGED ON CONFIDENTIALITY	
5 Your client's leader or HR asks for details about your client and your coaching sessions (e.g., confidential information).	Chapter 1: Putting Your Best Foot Forward Chapter 2: Starting Strong
6 Your client's leader or HR asks for a copy of your client's assessment report(s).	Chapter 1: Putting Your Best Foot Forward Chapter 3: Building Awareness
7 You have existing relationships in an organization, so individuals feel they can reach out to discuss current client work or provide input.	Chapter 1: Putting Your Best Foot Forward Chapter 2: Starting Strong
YOUR CLIENT IS RESISTING ASSESSMENT	
8 A client's sponsor says there is not enough progress.	Chapter 1: Putting Your Best Foot Forward Chapter 2: Starting Strong Chapter 3: Building Awareness
9 Your client fears what a 360 assessment might signal to others (e.g., that they are not an effective leader).	Chapter 1: Putting Your Best Foot Forward Chapter 2: Starting Strong Chapter 3: Building Awareness
10 The organization is concerned about rating fatigue amongst stakeholders.	Chapter 1: Putting Your Best Foot Forward Chapter 2: Starting Strong Chapter 3: Building Awareness
11 The client doesn't want to collect progress feedback from anyone at the end of the coaching.	Chapter 1: Putting Your Best Foot Forward Chapter 2: Starting Strong Chapter 7: Finishing Strong

ESTABLISHING THE THROUGH LINE

	STICKY SITUATION	WHERE WE COVER IT
	MANAGING THE PROCESS SO IT DOESN'T MANAGE YOU	
12	The client and/or sponsor want more 360 participants than are included in the Statement of Work.	Chapter 3: Building Awareness
13	The assessment process is significantly delayed by scheduling issues and the client is eager to move forward.	Chapter 2: Starting Strong Chapter 3: Building Awareness
14	The client organization is asking you to use an assessment in which you're not certified.	Chapter 3: Building Awareness
	YOUR CLIENT IS RESISTING OR STRUGGLING WITH THEIR LEADERSHIP VISION, GOAL SETTING, OR COACHING PLANS	
15	The client is delaying or resisting creating their vision, goals and/or a development plan.	Chapter 4: Charting the Course
16	The client is struggling to create vision, goals and/or a development plan.	Chapter 4: Charting the Course
17	The client is having a hard time defining success metrics.	Chapter 4: Charting the Course
18	The client drafts goals in their coaching plan that don't align with the feedback or aren't what the sponsor wants.	Chapter 3: Building Awareness Chapter 4: Charting the Course

ESTABLISHING THE THROUGH LINE

	STICKY SITUATION	WHERE WE COVER IT
	You're Questioning Your Client's Commitment	
19	The client is difficult to schedule or regularly cancels coaching meetings.	Chapter 2: Starting Strong Chapter 6: Pausing to Check Connection
20	The client is unresponsive to your emails and/or calls.	Chapter 2: Starting Strong Chapter 6: Pausing to Check Connection
	You're Working Harder Than The Client	
21	Your client expects you to set the agenda for coaching sessions.	Chapter 2: Starting Strong Chapter 6: Pausing to Check Connection
22	Your client expects you to provide solutions.	Chapter 2: Starting Strong Chapter 6: Pausing to Check Connection
23	You don't signal the end of the engagement soon enough and your client finds it abrupt/upsetting.	Chapter 2: Starting Strong Chapter 6: Pausing to Check Connection
	You Know You're Not At Your Best In Coaching Sessions	
24	You feel chronically unprepared or underprepared for coaching sessions.	Chapter 5: Being Intentional Chapter 8: Your Presence Is an Intervention
25	You have trouble maintaining presence in coaching sessions.	Chapter 5: Being Intentional Chapter 8: Your Presence Is an Intervention
26	Your coaching is suffering because you are overextended.	Chapter 5: Being Intentional Chapter 8: Your Presence Is an Intervention

MAKING PROGRESS

STICKY SITUATION	WHERE WE COVER IT
You're Concerned That Coaching Feels Stalled	
27 Coaching is feeling heavy and focused on what is wrong with the client.	Chapter 4: Charting the Course
28 Client feels stuck or not making forward progress fast enough.	Chapter 3: Building Awareness Chapter 4: Charting the Course
29 You feel like you're not getting traction; or your client cycles without forward progress.	Chapter 3: Building Awareness Chapter 4: Charting the Course Chapter 5: Being Intentional Chapter 6: Pausing to Check Connection
You're Dealing With a Challenging Sponsor	
30 You are having trouble engaging the client's sponsor (can't get sponsor meetings on calendar; client isn't getting informal feedback from sponsor).	Chapter 1: Putting Your Best Foot Forward Chapter 2: Starting Strong Chapter 6: Pausing to Check Connection
31 Organizational changes significantly impact your client's coaching goals mid-engagement.	Chapter 6: Pausing to Check Connection
32 The sponsor wants to outsource providing feedback to you instead of providing it directly.	Chapter 1: Putting Your Best Foot Forward Chapter 2: Starting Strong Chapter 6: Pausing to Check Connection
33 The sponsor wants to have a 1:1 meeting with you and then have you deliver their message(s) to the client.	Chapter 1: Putting Your Best Foot Forward Chapter 2: Starting Strong Chapter 3: Building Awareness Chapter 6: Pausing to Check Connection

MAKING PROGRESS

	STICKY SITUATION	WHERE WE COVER IT
	YOUR STRONG FINISH IS FALLING FLAT	
34	A client's sponsor says there is not enough progress	Chapter 1: Putting Your Best Foot Forward Chapter 4: Charting the Course Chapter 6: Pausing to Check Connection
35	Too much time has elapsed between your last coaching meeting and the closing meeting with the sponsor	Chapter 1: Putting Your Best Foot Forward Chapter 2: Starting Strong Chapter 6: Pausing to Check Connection Chapter 7: Finishing Strong
36	You had a closing meeting with your client but not with the sponsor	Chapter 1: Putting Your Best Foot Forward Chapter 2: Starting Strong Chapter 6: Pausing to Check Connection Chapter 7: Finishing Strong
37	The engagement has ended without any closing meeting	Chapter 1: Putting Your Best Foot Forward Chapter 2: Starting Strong Chapter 6: Pausing to Check Connection Chapter 7: Finishing Strong

ENDING WITH MEANING

ICF & EMCC COMPETENCIES (2020)

Coaching competencies have been established by governance and thought leadership bodies in the field of coaching, including the International Coaching Federation (ICF) and the European Mentoring and Coaching Council (EMCC). *Do Your Best Coaching* helps coaches attend to the ICF and EMCC competencies, as outlined below.

ICF COMPETENCIES

ICF COMPETENCY	SUGGESTED CHAPTER
A. Foundation *1. Demonstrates Ethical Practice* Definition: Understands and consistently applies coaching ethics and standards of coaching 1. Demonstrates personal integrity and honesty in interactions with clients, sponsors and relevant stakeholders 2. Is sensitive to clients' identity, environment, experiences, values and beliefs 3. Uses language appropriate and respectful to clients, sponsors and relevant stakeholders 4. Abides by the ICF Code of Ethics and upholds the Core Values 5. Maintains confidentiality with client information per stakeholder agreements and pertinent laws 6. Maintains the distinctions between coaching, consulting, psychotherapy and other support professions 7. Refers clients to other support professionals, as appropriate	Establishing and maintaining confidentiality with sponsors and stakeholders: Chapter 1: Putting Your Best Foot Forward Chapter 2: Starting Strong Chapter 3: Building Awareness

ICF COMPETENCY	SUGGESTED CHAPTER

Foundation
2. *Embodies a Coaching Mindset*
Definition: Develops and maintains a mindset that is open, curious, flexible and client-centered
   1. Acknowledges that clients are responsible for their own choices
   2. Engages in ongoing learning and development as a coach
   3. Develops an ongoing reflective practice to enhance one's coaching
   4. Remains aware of and open to the influence of context and culture on self and others
   5. Uses awareness of self and one's intuition to benefit clients
   6. Develops and maintains the ability to regulate one's emotions
   7. Mentally and emotionally prepares for sessions
   8. Seeks help from outside sources when necessary
	Reflective practices and session preparation:
	
	Chapter 5: Being Intentional
	
	Chapter 8: Your Presence Is An Intervention
	
	Ongoing development: for Coaches:
	
	Chapter 9: You Are Your Own Best Tool

ICF COMPETENCY	SUGGESTED CHAPTER

B. Co-Creating the Relationship
3. Establishes and Maintains Agreements
Definition: Partners with the client and relevant stakeholders to create clear agreements about the coaching relationship, process, plans and goals. Establishes agreements for the overall coaching engagement as well as those for each coaching session.
   1. Explains what coaching is and is not and describes the process to the client and relevant stakeholders
   2. Reaches agreement about what is and is not appropriate in the relationship, what is and is not being offered, and the responsibilities of the client and relevant stakeholders
   3. Reaches agreement about the guidelines and specific parameters of the coaching relationship such as logistics, fees, scheduling, duration, termination, confidentiality and inclusion of others
   4. Partners with the client and relevant stakeholders to establish an overall coaching plan and goals
   5. Partners with the client to determine client-coach compatibility
   6. Partners with the client to identify or reconfirm what they want to accomplish in the session
   7. Partners with the client to define what the client believes they need to address or resolve to achieve what they want to accomplish in the session
	Guidance establishing and maintaining agreements across the coaching engagement:
	
	Chapter 1: Putting Your Best Foot Forward
	
	Chapter 2: Starting Strong
	
	Chapter 3: Building Awareness
	
	Chapter 4: Charting the Course
	
	Chapter 5: Being Intentional
	
	Chapter 7: Finishing Strong

ICF COMPETENCY	SUGGESTED CHAPTER
8. Partners with the client to define or reconfirm measures of success for what the client wants to accomplish in the coaching engagement or individual session 9. Partners with the client to manage the time and focus of the session 10. Continues coaching in the direction of the client's desired outcome unless the client indicates otherwise 11. Partners with the client to end the coaching relationship in a way that honors the experience	Guidance establishing and maintaining agreements across the coaching engagement: Chapter 1: Putting Your Best Foot Forward Chapter 2: Starting Strong Chapter 3: Building Awareness Chapter 4: Charting the Course Chapter 5: Being Intentional Chapter 7: Finishing Strong

ICF COMPETENCY	SUGGESTED CHAPTER
B. Co-Creating the Relationship *4. Cultivates Trust and Safety* Definition: Partners with the client to create a safe, supportive environment that allows the client to share freely. Maintains a relationship of mutual respect and trust. 1. Seeks to understand the client within their context, which may include their identity, environment, experiences, values and beliefs 2. Demonstrates respect for the client's identity, perceptions, style and language and adapts one's coaching to the client 3. Acknowledges and respects the client's unique talents, insights and work in the coaching process 4. Shows support, empathy and concern for the client 5. Acknowledges and supports the client's expression of feelings, perceptions, concerns, beliefs and suggestions 6. Demonstrates openness and transparency as a way to display vulnerability and build trust with the client	Creating a trust-based relationship and the safe space for clients to do their work: Chapter 2: Starting Strong Chapter 5: Being Intentional

ICF COMPETENCY	SUGGESTED CHAPTER

B. Co-Creating the Relationship
5. Maintains Presence
Definition: Is fully conscious and present with the client, employing a style that is open, flexible, grounded and confident
   1. Remains focused, observant, empathetic and responsive to the client
   2. Demonstrates curiosity during the coaching process
   3. Manages one's emotions to stay present with the client
   4. Demonstrates confidence in working with strong client emotions during the coaching process
   5. Is comfortable working in a space of not knowing
   6. Creates or allows space for silence, pause or reflection
	Presence during specific points of the engagement:
	
	Chapter 3: Building Awareness
	
	Chapter 5: Being Intentional
	
	Developing coaching presence:
	
	Chapter 8: Your Presence Is an Intervention

ICF COMPETENCY	SUGGESTED CHAPTER

C. Communicating Effectively
6. Listens Actively
Definition: Focuses on what the client is and is not saying to fully understand what is being communicated in the context of the client systems and to support client self-expression
    1. Considers the client's context, identity, environment, experiences, values and beliefs to enhance understanding of what the client is communicating
    2. Reflects or summarizes what the client communicated to ensure clarity and understanding
    3. Recognizes and inquires when there is more to what the client is communicating
    4. Notices, acknowledges and explores the client's emotions, energy shifts, nonverbal cues or other behaviors
    5. Integrates the client's words, tone of voice and body language to determine the full meaning of what is being communicated
    6. Notices trends in the client's behaviors and emotions across sessions to discern themes and patterns
	Active listening:
	Chapter 2: Starting Strong
	Chapter 5: Being Intentional
	Chapter 8: Your Presence Is An Intervention

ICF COMPETENCY	SUGGESTED CHAPTER

C. Communicating Effectively
7. Evokes Awareness
Definition: Facilitates client insight and learning by using tools and techniques such as powerful questioning, silence, metaphor or analogy
    1. Considers client experience when deciding what might be most useful
    2. Challenges the client as a way to evoke awareness or insight
    3. Asks questions about the client, such as their way of thinking, values, needs, wants and beliefs
    4. Asks questions that help the client explore beyond current thinking
    5. Invites the client to share more about their experience in the moment
    6. Notices what is working to enhance client progress
    7. Adjusts the coaching approach in response to the client's needs
    8. Helps the client identify factors that influence current and future patterns of behavior, thinking or emotion
    9. Invites the client to generate ideas about how they can move forward and what they are willing or able to do
    10. Supports the client in reframing perspectives
    11. Shares observations, insights and feelings, without attachment, that have the potential to create new learning for the client
	Evoking awareness in clients by creating the right conditions:
	
	Chapter 3: Building Awareness
	
	Chapter 4: Charting the Course
	
	Chapter 5: Being Intentional
	
	Chapter 6: Pausing to Check Connection

ICF COMPETENCY	SUGGESTED CHAPTER
D. Cultivating Learning and Growth *8. Facilitates Client Growth* Definition: Partners with the client to transform learning and insight into action. Promotes client autonomy in the coaching process. 　1. Works with the client to integrate new awareness, insight or learning into their worldview and behaviors 　2. Partners with the client to design goals, actions and accountability measures that integrate and expand new learning 　3. Acknowledges and supports client autonomy in the design of goals, actions and methods of accountability 　4. Supports the client in identifying potential results or learning from identified action steps 　5. Invites the client to consider how to move forward, including resources, support and potential barriers 　6. Partners with the client to summarize learning and insight within or between sessions 　7. Celebrates the client's progress and successes 　8. Partners with the client to close the session	Using assessments to generate new learning: Chapter 3: Building Awareness Chapter 3+: 360° Assessments Designing goals and success measures: Chapter 4: Charting the Course Preparing clients for learning in and from sessions: Chapter 5: Being Intentional Recognizing and celebrating progress: Chapter 7: Finishing Strong

EMCC COMPETENCES
EIGHT COACHING / MENTORING COMPETENCE CATEGORIES

CATEGORY	DESCRIPTION	RECOMMENDED CHAPTER
1. Understanding Self	Demonstrates awareness of own values, beliefs and behaviours; recognises how these affect their practice and uses this self-awareness to manage their effectiveness in meeting the client's, and where relevant, the sponsor's objectives	Understanding self as coach and the impact on the coaching engagement: Chapter 5: Being Intentional Chapter 6: Pausing to Check Connection Chapter 7: Finishing Strong Chapter 8: Your Presence Is an Intervention Chapter 9: You Are Your Own Best Tool
2. Commitment to Self-Development	Explore and improve the standard of their practice and maintain the reputation of the profession	Ongoing development for Coaches: Chapter 9: You Are Your Own Best Tool
3. Managing the Contract	Establishes and maintains the expectations and boundaries of the mentoring/coaching contract with the client and, where appropriate, with sponsors	Expectations, boundaries, and contracting: Chapter 1: Putting Your Best Foot Forward Chapter 2: Starting Strong Chapter 4: Charting the Course Chapter 6: Pausing to Check Connection Chapter 7: Finishing Strong

CATEGORY	DESCRIPTION	RECOMMENDED CHAPTER
4. Building the Relationship	Skillfully builds and maintains an effective relationship with the client, and where appropriate, with the sponsor	Building and maintaining effective relationships over the course of the coaching engagement: Chapter 2: Starting Strong Chapter 5: Being Intentional Chapter 6: Pausing to Check Connection Chapter 7: Finishing Strong
5. Enabling Insight and Learning	Works with the client and sponsor to bring about insight and learning	Creating the container for client and sponsor insight and learning: Chapter 3: Building Awareness Chapter 4: Charting the Course Chapter 5: Being Intentional Chapter 6: Pausing to Check Connection Chapter 7: Finishing Strong
6. Outcome and Action Orientation	Demonstrates approach and uses the skills in supporting the client to make desired changes	Chapter 4: Charting the Course, Chapter 5: Being Intentional, Chapter 6: Pausing to Check Connection, and Chapter 7: Finishing Strong all support taking an outcome and action orientation to coaching work, working with clients to make their desired changes.

CATEGORY	DESCRIPTION	RECOMMENDED CHAPTER
7. Use of Models and Techniques	Applies models and tools, techniques, and ideas beyond the core communication skills in order to bring about insight and learning	Using tools and techniques beyond core communication skills: Chapter 3: Building Awareness Chapter 5: Being Intentional Bringing about insight at the mid-engagement and closing points: Chapter 6: Pausing to Check Connection Chapter 7: Finishing Strong
8. Evaluation	Gathers information on the effectiveness of own practice and contributes to establishing a culture of evaluation of outcomes.	Setting an engagement up to include the expectation and explanation of evaluation: Chapter 1: Putting Your Best Foot Forward Chapter 2: Starting Strong Soliciting feedback for the coach as well as the client: Chapter 5: Being Intentional Chapter 6: Pausing to Check Connection Chapter 7: Finishing Strong Stepping back to evaluate one's work as a coach: Chapter 9: You Are Your Own Best Tool

INDEX

Note: Examples of coaching conversations are listed under "coaching vignettes."

ABOUT US

JULIE HESS

For more than 25 years, Julie Hess has worked with leaders, teams, and organizations to achieve breakthrough results.

Julie began her career in the industrial plastics industry, working with global clients to solve complex design and manufacturing challenges. During this time she identified an untapped market for existing materials that she subsequently developed into her firm's fastest-growing business unit.

Later, she took her passion for problem-solving into the world of corporate and organizational strategy, first at consulting firm CSC Index and later as an executive in Motorola's Leadership and Organization Effectiveness Group. It was here that Julie developed her passion for coaching, which led her to complete her initial coaching certification at the Hudson Institute of Santa Barbara, a pioneer in coach education and development. In 2001, Julie founded Catalyst Consulting and has continuously led and grown the practice since.

Today, Julie divides her time between her executive coaching practice and supporting the development of other coaches as a Coach Supervisor and educator. Her broad background enables her to fully appreciate the challenges that her coaching clients and their organizations face. Julie has worked with clients in a broad range of industries including technology, healthcare, consumer packaged goods, pharmaceuticals, hospitality, automotive, financial services, professional services, and real estate. She is known as an authentic, thoughtful, and direct partner to her clients, helping them to achieve the growth they desire.

Julie holds an MBA from the Kellogg Graduate School of Business and a Master of Engineering Management from the McCormick School of Engineering at Northwestern University, and a BS in Business Administration from DePaul University. She earned her diploma in Coach Supervision from the Coaching Supervision Academy and holds a PCC from the International Coach Federation.

Julie lives in Chicago, Illinois, and Naples, Florida, with her best coach, her husband Dan, and their two dogs Noodle and Mousse.

LAURA DALEY

Laura is an executive coach, leadership advisor, and strategy consultant with more than 25 years of experience. Over the past decade, she has coached hundreds of executives in industries including private equity, technology, financial services, biopharma, and nonprofits. Laura is direct and empathetic, combining practical business perspective with an appreciation for the challenges leaders face as they develop new ways of thinking and working.

Having experienced all sides of coaching, Laura brings a broad perspective and appreciation for her clients and their organizational systems. At Spencer Stuart, as Vice President of Learning & Development, she supported firm leaders through coaching. In building The Goodstone Group, she grew the coach network and partnered with clients to match coaches to their needs. Today, Laura serves as an external coach and advisor, working with executives, leadership teams, and coaches-in-training.

Laura's first career was management consulting, working for Katzenbach Partners, Scient, Gemini Consulting, and American Management Systems. She consulted across industries and functions, worked with start-ups, midsize companies, and multinationals, and traveled the world for clients in North America, Europe, Africa, and Asia. She holds an MBA with honors from UCLA Anderson, a BA with honors in Economics and International Relations from Cornell University, and a PCC from the International Coach Federation. She studied at the Hudson Institute of Coaching, the Graduate Institute, Geneva, and HEC Paris.

Laura enjoys learning and drawing inspiration from her husband, Alec, and daughter, Maddie, as well as her clients, movement, and travel.

Printed in Great Britain
by Amazon